ONCE
IN CHRIST
+++
IN CHRIST
FOREVER

Some books by William MacDonald

Armageddon Soon?
Believer's Bible Commentary
Christ Loved the Church
Enjoying Ecclesiastes
Enjoy Your Bible
Ephesians: Mystery of the Church
1 Peter: Faith Tested, Future Triumphant
God's Answers to Man's Questions
Grasping for Shadows
Here's the Difference
Lord, Break Me
My Heart, My Life, My All
One Day at a Time
Our God is Wonderful
True Discipleship
Wonders of God
Worlds Apart

ONCE IN CHRIST

✝ ✝ ✝

IN CHRIST FOREVER

With more than 100 Biblical reasons
why a true believer cannot be lost

William MacDonald

GOSPEL FOLIO PRESS
304 Killaly St., West Port Colborne, ON L3K 6A6

Published by Gospel Folio Press
304 Killaly St., West Port Colborne, ON L3K 6A6

Abbreviations

NKJV	New King James Version
KJV	King James Version
NIV	New International Version
TEV	Today's English Version
TLB	The Living Bible

ISBN 1-882701-43-7

Cover design by J. B. Nicholson, Jr.

Printed in the United States of America

What from Christ the soul can sever,
Bound by everlasting bands?
Once in Him, in Him forever,
Thus the eternal cov'nant stands.
None shall pluck thee, none shall pluck thee
From the Savior's mighty hands!

—JOHN KENT

Contents

1
Once in Christ, in Christ Forever

From the early days of the Church, this crucial question has been debated: Is a believer saved eternally, or can he lose his salvation through sin? On the one side are the Calvinists,[1] who believe in the perseverance of the saints[2], or, better, the perseverance of Christ. On the other are the Arminians[3] who teach that salvation is conditional. This doctrinal dispute will continue as long as the Church is on earth.

To be perfectly frank, there are Scriptures which seem to support each side. There are verses, which taken in isolation, confirm a Methodist or Pentecostal, for example, in believing what is sometimes called "the falling away doctrine." And there are plenty of other passages which assure Baptists and many other believers that their salvation is secure forever.

You will find true believers in both camps. John Wesley, a strong Arminian, and Charles Spurgeon, a strong Calvinist, held opposite views on this issue, yet who would doubt the reality of their conversion experiences? Both were true Christians. Neither side can claim a monopoly on the new birth.

And neither side can claim a monopoly on holiness. The godly lives of men and women from both schools of thought should make us careful not to dismiss any of them as heretics or speak unkindly of them.

Therefore, in discussing the matter with one another, it is useless to try to prove our case by pointing to prominent Christians. The other side can do that just as effectively. Even quoting these leaders is only of value if their words are based on Scripture and help to illustrate it.

Another futile way of arguing is by appealing to human experience. As if to settle the matter once for all, we often hear the pronouncement, "Well, I knew a man who...." But this overlooks the fact that there are all kinds of human experience. And, even more important, it forgets that spiritual experiences must conform to the Word of God in order to be valued as evidence.

In forming our convictions on the subject, we must approach the Scriptures *humbly.* There are problems on both sides of the question of security, conditional or unconditional. We should face that fact honestly.

We should face the Scriptures *prayerfully,* asking the Holy Spirit to reveal the truth to us as we study them in detail.

And we should face the Scriptures *objectively.* Instead of merely searching for arguments to support our preconceived position, we should be constantly open to the Spirit's teaching. This is admittedly difficult. Once we have publicly adopted a stance on any controversial issue, it's difficult to change when it means losing face!

In studying objectively, we will follow these simple guidelines.

1. A verse must be studied in the light of its immediate context. If the context is about service, we shouldn't apply it to salvation.

2. A verse must be interpreted in the light of all the rest of the Word of God. No one passage, rightly understood, will contradict dozens of other verses.

3. Definitions should include every major use of the word.

4. A doctrine must be based on all that the Bible teaches on that subject.

It's clear from the title of this book that the author holds the view that the believer is eternally secure. In the rest of the book, he seeks to set forth the Scriptural basis for this belief. But he also seeks to explain those Bible passages which are most commonly used to prove that a Christian can lose his salvation.

Some will wonder why we quote so few Old Testament verses to support eternal security, and why little space is given to explain Old Testament verses that are used to support conditional salvation. Why is this?

The reason is that these are not subjects that are clearly developed in the Old Testament. For example, there are very few passages that deal with life after death in heaven. There is no question that Jewish believers were saved by faith in the Lord. And I have no doubt that this was an eternal salvation. Although the Lord's people had a heavenly hope (Heb. 11:16), their main expectation was the Messiah's kingdom here on earth. The whole subject of the hereafter was shrouded in mists of obscurity. That gives special meaning to Paul's announcement that "our Savior Jesus Christ brought life and immortality to light through the gospel" (2 Tim. 1:10). Truths that existed only in seed form in the Old Testament are fully developed in the New.

So that no one thinks we're trying to avoid difficulties by not discussing Old Testament passages, we should mention that some of the definitive works on conditional security *also* confine their attention to the New Testament.

ENDNOTES

1 Calvinists follow the teachings of French-born John Calvin (1509-1564). He became the chief leader of the Reformation in Switzerland and placed a strong emphasis on God's sovereignty.

2 The perseverance of the saints does not mean that they are saved by enduring, but that if they are truly saved, they will go on to the end. For anyone to say, "It would be presumption for me to say that I am saved," shows that he is depending in whole or in part on his own performance. If God says that anyone who has the Son has life right now (1 Jn. 5:12), it is not presumption for a believer to say so. To deny it is to make God a liar.

3 Arminians, by contrast to Calvinists, follow teachings developed by Dutch theologian Jacobus Arminius (1560-1609), who emphasized man's free will as the primary factor in salvation.

2
Shall Never Perish

One of the most conclusive statements on the eternal security of the believer is John 10:27-29. Anyone who reads it can be excused for believing that a person who is born again is eternally secure. In fact, it is difficult to see how anyone could reach a different conclusion. Let's examine the passage phrase by phrase and enjoy the assurance it gives.

My sheep hear My voice, and I know them, and they follow Me. And I give them eternal life, and they shall never perish; neither shall anyone snatch them out of My hand. My Father, who has given them to Me, is greater than all; and no one is able to snatch them out of My Father's hand (Jn. 10:27-29).

My sheep hear My voice, and I know them, and they follow Me. This is a declarative statement. It tells us who the sheep of Christ are. They are people who hear His Word, they respond to His voice in the gospel and are saved.

He knows them. He recognizes them as His own. He distinguishes them from non-believers and from false professors. He can tell where there is genuine faith when none of us might suspect it, as in the case of Lot (2 Pet. 2:7) and of Samson (Heb. 11:32).

They follow Him. This is not a condition. He does *not* say that they are his sheep *if* they follow Him or *as long as* they follow Him. Rather, this is what characterizes the true believer. He characteristically follows Christ (see Jn. 10:4-5). I say "characteristically" because nobody does it perfectly. We are all "prone to wander...prone to leave the God [we] love." But the Shepherd assumes the responsibility of restoring the wandering sheep.

15

I give them eternal life. Again we have an unconditional promise, no strings attached. Eternal life is a gift. A gift with conditions is no gift at all! Anyone who has committed himself or herself to the Lord Jesus Christ for his soul's salvation can know, on the authority of the Word of God, that he has eternal life.

They shall never perish. Think for a moment of the consequences if one sheep of Christ ever perished. Christ would then have gone back on His promise! He would no longer be God. The Trinity would cease. The Bible would be undependable. We would still be in our sins. It can't happen, because fulfillment of the promise depends on Christ alone and not on His sheep.

Neither shall anyone snatch them out of My hand. Jesus Christ, the eternal Son of God, guarantees that His sheep are held in His hand and that no one can remove them by force.

Arminians argue, "No one *else* can pluck them away, but a believer *himself* can do it." This is bizarre—that a true Christian has more power than anyone else in the universe. No one—and that includes the sheep—can remove himself from the Shepherd's strong grip.

My Father, who has given them to me, is greater than all. To further emphasize the security of the Christian, Jesus states that true believers are the Father's gift to the Son. If one believer could pluck himself out of Christ's hand, then it is conceivable that all His sheep could do it. They not only could; they probably would. In that case, God's gift to His Son would disappear. What kind of a gift would that be? Certainly it would be unworthy of the Father.

No, the Father is greater than all, that is, greater than all other powers in the universe, and certainly greater than the strength of a sheep. The "all" includes the sheep.

No one is able to snatch them out of My Father's hand. In view of such marvelous assurance, it is perverse that people should object that a true sheep of Christ should decide that he doesn't want to be a sheep any longer, and could thus remove himself from his Father's hand.

The argument will not stand. The words "no one" are absolute.

They do not allow for any exception. The inspired text doesn't say "no one except a sheep of Christ himself"—and neither should we.

3
By Grace Through Faith

Whenever I think of eternal security, one of the first passages that comes to mind is Ephesians 2:8-10.

For by grace you have been saved through faith, and that not of yourselves; it is the gift of God, not of works, lest anyone should boast. For we are His workmanship, created in Christ Jesus for good works, which God prepared beforehand that we should walk in them (Eph. 2:8-10).

Salvation is by grace. That means that no one deserves it. It is God's unmerited favor to those who deserve eternal punishment. It is everything for nothing to one who deserves nothing. It is a gift which, once given, will never be retracted (Rom. 11:29). The gift is unconditional. Add conditions and it becomes debt, not grace, and yet God is indebted to nobody (Rom. 11:35). Grace that has conditions is no grace at all. The only way a person can be sure of his salvation is when it is by grace (Rom. 4:16).

In Ephesians 2:8-9, Paul is reminding the Ephesians that it was by grace that they had been saved. When they had by faith received Jesus Christ as Lord and Savior, they had been saved and were still saved. There were no strings attached. It was a spiritual event with continuing results. No legal requirements had been laid on them with threat of possible eternal damnation. There is no "if" after the word "saved"; it is conspicuous by its absence.

God gives salvation as a free gift, but the sinner must receive it. That is where faith comes in. Faith is implicit confidence in the Word of God. The Lord does not coerce people. He doesn't take anyone to heaven who doesn't want to be there. To be saved, each one must receive Jesus Christ by a definite act of faith. Faith is not meritorious and therefore it leaves no place for boasting. It is not the *amount* of faith that matters but the *Object* of that faith.

When Paul adds "and that not of yourselves," some people understandably think that he is speaking of faith. They then go on to conclude that God gives faith to some and not to others. But that is a strange conclusion. The antecedent of "that not of yourselves" is salvation by grace through faith.[1] What Paul is saying is that there is nothing meritorious a person can do to be saved or even to contribute to his salvation. All the merit is in Christ, none in the believer.

As we have seen, salvation is the free gift of God. When He makes an unconditional promise of eternal life, no restrictions can be added later to annul that promise. When He gives a gift, no later law can cancel that gift.

Salvation is "not of works, lest anyone should boast." There is nothing meritorious a person can do in order to obtain it.[2] Otherwise heaven would be populated with people bragging about their own attainments. Salvation is the Lord's work from start to finish. Man is only the fortunate recipient. He is, and ever will be, "only a sinner saved by grace." Grace and works are mutually exclusive (Rom. 11:6).

Verse 10 emphasizes that works are not the means of salvation; they are the result. They are not the root but the fruit. We are not saved *by* good works but *for* good works. This is the purpose of our creation in Christ Jesus. Before we were saved, God prepared good works that we should accomplish in our lives as believers.

Down through the centuries, millions of people have rested their eternal welfare on the truth of God in these verses in Ephesians 2, and not one has been disappointed or failed to reach heaven at last.

ENDNOTES

1   As in Spanish, French, and Latin, the original text uses nouns and adjectives that are masculine, feminine, or (in Greek) neuter. Since the words for *grace* and *faith* are both feminine in Greek, if Paul had wanted that to refer back to one of them, he would have used a feminine form. But he used a neuter word, referring to the whole preceding clause *by grace you have been saved through faith.*

2   In one sense, even faith is a work (Jn. 6:28-29), but it is not a meritorious work. It is simply believing Someone who can only say what is true.

4

The Believer's Security in Romans 8

Nowhere in the Bible is the security of the believer taught more clearly and thoroughly than in the eighth chapter of Romans. Paul piles truth upon truth to show that nothing and no one can rob a Christian of his or her eternal destiny with Christ in heaven.

In verses 29 and 30 the apostle traces five steps in God's great program for us from eternity to eternity.

For whom He foreknew, He also predestined to be conformed to the image of His Son, that He might be the firstborn among many brethren. Moreover whom He predestined, these He also called; whom He called, these He also justified; and whom He justified, these He also glorified.

He foreknew us. This means more than that He knew in eternity past who would choose Christ as Savior. God also foreknew Israel (Rom. 11:2). This means that He *chose* that nation as His earthly people.[1] It certainly doesn't mean that the people of Israel chose Him, because their history shows that they didn't. It was all of grace. Yet God's foreknowledge doesn't absolve man of responsibility.[2]

He predestined us. God's goal was that those whom He foreknew would be like His Son morally, spiritually, and physically, in a glorified body.[3] All who believe on the Lord Jesus are sons of God. But He has one *unique* Son. And the Father has determined that Jesus will have the place of highest honor (firstborn) among His other sons and daughters.

He called us. His foreknowledge and predestination took place before the foundations of the world. His call took place in time. In a real sense, He calls everyone who hears the preaching of the gospel (Rev. 22:17). But here the apostle is thinking of the effectiveness of that call in those who respond to the gospel and are converted.

He justified us. When we repent and believe, God declares us to be righteous. He acquits us of every charge against us. It is more than being pronounced not guilty. He actually imputes or reckons righteousness to us. We stand before Him, clothed in His own righteousness.

This is not a verdict that is conditional on our performance. It is a once-for-all declaration that the believing sinner is cleared of every charge. Because the sacrificial work of Christ atoned for all his sins from birth to death, God, the Judge, cannot find a single sin in the record for which to punish him with eternal death.

He glorified us. This is the clincher in the five-linked chain of argument! The Holy Spirit daringly puts the verb in the past tense—He glorified us—even though our present infirmities remind us all too vividly that we have not yet reached the glorified state. The point is that if a person has been justified, his glorification is as certain as if it had already taken place.

Paul is not through. In the rest of the chapter, he drives home the unassailable position of the person who is in Christ, then explores the universe for anything that can separate him from God's love—and comes up empty.

What then shall we say to these things? If God is for us, who can be against us? He who did not spare His own Son, but delivered Him up for us all, how shall He not with Him also freely give us all things? Who shall bring a charge against God's elect? It is God who justifies. Who is he who condemns? It is Christ who died, and furthermore is also risen, who is even at the right hand of God, who also makes intercession for us. Who shall separate us from the love of Christ? Shall tribulation, or distress, or persecution, or famine, or nakedness, or peril, or sword? As it is written, "For Your sake we are killed all day long; we are accounted as sheep for the slaughter." Yet in all these things we are more than conquerors through Him who loved us. For I am persuaded that neither death nor life, nor angels nor principalities nor powers, nor things present nor things to come, nor height nor depth, nor any other created thing, shall be able to separate us from the love of God which is in Christ Jesus our Lord (Rom. 8:31-39).

The apostle here presses home five more arguments to demonstrate that no one could possibly be more safe eternally than the person who has trusted Christ as his Savior.

God is for us. Since God is on our side, our opponents are God's opponents. Nothing can be more futile than fighting against God. No attacks against us can be successful in the long run.[4]

The greater includes the lesser. God has already made the greatest sacrifice by sending His Son to earth. And He has already given the greatest gift by delivering Him up for us all. It follows that with Him He will freely give us all things. And "all things" includes the gift of perfect, complete, and eternal salvation. Since it is a free gift, it is unconditional and not probational. Everything depends on the generosity of the Giver and not on the merit of the recipient.

No one can accuse. The idea is that no one can do it justifiably or successfully. The devil accuses us day and night (Rev. 12:10). But what difference does it make when the righteousness of God has been put to our account?

> *What though the accuser roar*
> *Of ills that I have done?*
> *I know them well and thousands more;*
> *Jehovah findeth none.* —Samuel W. Gandy

No one can condemn. The reason is that Christ has died to bear our condemnation on the cross. He is risen, a proof that God is fully satisfied with His finished work on our behalf. He is at the right hand of God as our High Priest and Advocate. He intercedes for us, assuring us of His power to keep us secure.

There is no condemnation for those who are in Christ Jesus.

Their penalty has been paid, and God does not require payment twice.

Since Thou hast my discharge procured,
And freely in my place endured
The whole of wrath divine,
Payment God will not twice demand,
First at my bleeding Surety's hand,
And then again at mine.

—Augustus M. Toplady

There is no condemnation, there is no hell for me!
The torment and the fire my eyes shall never see!
For me there is no sentence, for me death has no sting,
For Christ, my Lord, who saved me,
    will shield me with His wing!

—Paul Gerhardt

Nothing can separate. In a full, deep outburst, Paul ransacks time and space for anything that might separate a believer from the love of God which is in Christ Jesus our Lord. The search proves fruitless.

Notice the expression "nor any other created thing." Some argue that while no other creature can separate a believer, he can separate himself. This is not a worthy way to handle the Scriptures. The believer himself is included in the phrase "any other created thing." The Holy Spirit is insistent that nothing and nobody, including the believer himself, can separate him from God's love.

What further need have we for argument? What further need do we have of witnesses?

ENDNOTES

1   The choosing of Israel was not to salvation but to a *role* in accomplishing the purposes of God. Many elect ones in Israel were not the true Israel (Rom. 9:6), that is, they did not have a living relationship with God. Since it was possible for Israelites (like Korah, for example) to be lost, can those "chosen...in Him" (Eph. 1:4) be lost? No, Israel's election was based merely on physical birth; the Christian's election is based on the new birth. As such, we have everlasting life and can never perish (Jn. 3:16). *ed.*

2   As in any human love relationship (God's unchangeable love is the concluding theme of Romans 8), if a man chooses a woman to be the object of his love, does it follow that she then does not have a choice? She also chooses to love him, and the New Testament is full of such calls to "come," "receive," "believe," "trust," etc. *ed.*

3   As noted, predestination does not have to do with *where* those who receive Christ will be (heaven or hell), but *what,* by God's grace, we will be (see also Jn. 1:11-12). *ed.*

4   Harassed by enemies within Geneva and by anti-reformation forces surrounding Switzerland, Calvin made Romans 8:31 what we might today call his "life verse."

5
Much More

For when we were still without strength, in due time Christ died
for the ungodly. For scarcely for a righteous man will one die;
yet perhaps for a good man someone would even dare to die. But
God demonstrates His own love toward us, in that while we were
still sinners, Christ died for us. Much more then, having now
been justified by His blood, we shall be saved from wrath
through Him. For if when we were enemies we were reconciled
to God through the death of His Son, much more, having been
reconciled, we shall be saved by His life. And not only that, but
we also rejoice in God through our Lord Jesus Christ, through
whom we have now received the reconciliation (Rom. 5:6-11).

The words "much more" deserve special attention in this passage
on the security of the believer. Here is the flow of argument:

Christ died for us when we were neither righteous nor good. Actually, we were without strength, ungodly, and sinners. In other
words, we had nothing to commend us to God. There was nothing
in us to draw out His love. On the contrary, there were strong reasons why He, the Holy One, should *not* love us. And yet it was
when we were in that condition of utter unworthiness that God
loved us and Christ died for us!

That leads us to the first "much more." If the Lord loved us when
we were so unlovable, much more will He save us from eternal
wrath now that we are justified by His blood. If He went to such
enormous cost to reckon us righteous, will He ever let us slip out of
His grip? Will He ever let us go? The question requires a resound-
ing "No!"

In addition to all our other liabilities, we were enemies of God. You would think that, in itself, that would bar us from any chance of receiving mercy from Him. But it was while we were His bitter foes that He reconciled us to Himself by the death of His Son.

And now the second "much more." Through the work of the Lord Jesus at Calvary, God has provided a way by which we might be reconciled to Himself. When we repent and believe in Christ, the enmity is removed. "Therefore having been justified by faith, we have peace with God through our Lord Jesus Christ" (Rom. 5:1). If the cost of our reconciliation was the death of God's Son, much more, having been reconciled, we shall be saved by His life. If Christ died for us when we were enemies, will He let us perish now that we are His friends?

But how are we saved by His life? That does not mean His life as a Man while here on earth. It means His present life at the right hand of God in heaven where He is our Advocate, Intercessor, High Priest, and Shepherd.

Here we should remind ourselves that salvation has three tenses.

Past. *We were saved* from the eternal penalty of sin when we trusted Christ. When He died, all our sins were future and He paid the penalty for them all.

Present. We *are being saved* from the power of sin. This is what is meant by the words "we are saved by His life." If our day by day security depended on our miserable attainments, we would all be lost. We are preserved by His intercession. We are kept because He pleads our cause. We are secure because He restores us when we wander.

Future. We *will be saved* from the very presence of sin. This refers, of course, to the time when we are in heaven, where we will be free from every last vestige of sin.

The argument is conclusive. If God saved us from wrath by giving His Son to die for us, He will never let us suffer that wrath. If we were reconciled to God by the blood of Christ when we were enemies, He will ensure our continued salvation through the present ministry of Christ on our behalf.

6
The Spirit of Assurance

No discussion of the eternal security of the believer is comprehensive without including the ministry of the Holy Spirit. He Himself is the guarantee that every genuine believer will reach heaven at last.

Every child of God has the Holy Spirit. "Now if anyone does not have the Spirit of Christ, he is not His" (Rom. 8:9). Jesus promised the disciples that the Spirit of truth would be in them (Jn. 14:17). And Paul reminds us that our bodies are the temple of the Holy Spirit (1 Cor. 6:19).

Once the Spirit takes residence in a believer, He remains forever. In promising Him, the Savior said, "And I will pray the Father, and He will give you another Helper, that He may abide with you *forever* (Jn. 14:16). It is an unconditional promise. There is no suggestion that the Spirit could be grieved away.

The Third Person of the Trinity is given to the Christian as a seal:

[God] also has sealed us... (2 Cor 1:22).

...in whom also, having believed, you were sealed with the Holy Spirit of promise (Eph. 1:13b).

The seal speaks of ownership and security. Anyone who has the Spirit is God's possession. In this sense, the seal is similar to the brand mark on cattle or the dye mark on sheep. They identify the owner.

As the seal, the Holy Spirit guarantees the eternal preservation of the child of God.

And do not grieve the Holy Spirit of God, by whom you were sealed for the day of redemption (Eph. 4:30).

The day of redemption is the time when we will receive our glorified bodies. Just as surely as we have the seal, so certain is it that we will reach heaven at last.

The Holy Spirit is also given to God's children as an earnest or deposit.

[God] also has... given us the Spirit in our hearts as a guarantee (2 Cor. 1:22).

Now He who has prepared us for this very thing is God, who also has given us the Spirit as a guarantee (2 Cor. 5:5).

The guarantee is a down payment or a pledge. In purchasing a house, a person makes a first installment as a guarantee that the full amount will follow. When a couple gets engaged, the engagement ring is a pledge that marriage will follow.[1] As a guarantee, the Holy Spirit is God's promise to the believer that the full inheritance will follow. When we are saved, our spirits and souls are redeemed, but we are still in bodies that are subject to sickness and death. The redemption of the body and our home in heaven are still future. But the guarantee of the Spirit makes them absolutely certain. Paul makes this clear in Ephesians 1:14:

[The Holy Spirit of promise] is the guarantee of our inheritance until the redemption of the purchased possession, to the praise of His glory.

Another figure that is used in connection with the Spirit is that of firstfruits. In the Old Testament, a farmer took a handful of the earliest ripened grain and offered it to God in gratitude for the crop that would yet be harvested. Paul sees a spiritual application here:

Not only that, but we also who have the firstfruits of the Spirit, even we ourselves groan within ourselves, eagerly waiting for the adoption, the redemption of our body (Rom. 8:23).

We already have the firstfruits of the Spirit, such as the seal and first installment which we have discussed. But we long for the full fruition of His ministry in our lives, that is, the redemption of our bodies.

There is a distinctive way in which those who have the firstfruits of the Spirit suffer: We groan within ourselves, eagerly waiting for the adoption, the redemption of the body (see v. 23). So the "if" of Romans 8:17 does not express the possible ordeal of a select few, but the inescapable privilege of *all* God's people.

We were saved in this hope, the hope of eternal life with the Lord in heaven. But there is no element of uncertainty in this hope[2] because it is founded on the Word of God, the surest thing in the universe.

One other ministry of the Spirit needs mention, that is, the anointing. In 1 John 2:27, the apostle John writes:

But the anointing which you have received from Him abides in you, and you do not need that anyone teach you; but as the same anointing teaches you concerning all things, and is true, and is not a lie, and just as it has taught you, you will abide in Him.

The anointing here refers to the teaching ministry of the Holy Spirit, the ability He gives believers to discern between truth and error. Highlight the words "abides in you." The anointing does not come and then leave! It remains in the child of God because the Holy Spirit remains.

In fact, all the ministries of the Helper we have mentioned are designed to fill the Christian with deepest assurance concerning his eternal destiny in heaven. There is no suggestion here that any genuine child of God can forfeit or lose his or her salvation. The Holy Spirit guarantees that we will eventually receive our glorified bodies. Our eternal security and the Holy Spirit stand together. Only if the Spirit could fail could our security fail.

33

ENDNOTES

1 It is a fascinating fact that the very word Paul uses here in first century Greek has come to mean "engagement ring" in modern Greek.

2 It is worth noting that the word Paul uses for "hope" is generally stronger than our English word.

7
In Christ

As soon as anyone believes on the Lord Jesus, he is "in Christ." This refers to the position of favor God gives him. Jehovah no longer looks on him in all his unworthiness, but now He sees him clothed in all the worthiness of Christ.

In Christ the believer was foreknown, chosen, and predestinated before the foundation of the world (Rom. 8:28-30). Obviously this was before he had done either good or evil. Since God is omniscient, He knew in advance all that the chosen one would ever do. And yet He chose him and predestined him to be like His Son forever. If the believer could ever lose his salvation, what the Lord had decreed would never happen. And His choice would have been a mistake. But it is impossible for God to be mistaken.

In Christ the believer is forgiven, pardoned, redeemed, and freed from all condemnation. If his continued salvation depends on his performance, then God would have to revoke those benefits which He had conferred completely apart from the person's own merit. In fact, they were conferred in spite of mountainous demerit. Would God change His mind in this matter? It is impossible!

In Christ the believer is positionally righteous. Actually, he is clothed with the righteousness of God (2 Cor. 5:21). He is not righteous in himself, but God's righteousness has been imputed to his account. That and that alone is what makes him fit for "the inheritance of the saints in light."

It is in Christ that a believing sinner is accepted (Eph. 1:6). In Christ He is as near to God as Christ is, and as dear to God as well (Jn. 17:23). Before he could ever lose this privileged position, the Lord Jesus would have to lose His acceptance with God the Father. Nothing could be more unthinkable.

In Christ God's child is complete (Col. 2:10). Christ is his total fitness for heaven. Christ's merit and the believer's fitness stand together.

Not only is the believer in Christ; Christ is in the believer. The union is so complete that the apostle Paul can say, "He who is joined to the Lord is one Spirit with Him" (1 Cor. 6:17). Nothing can be closer, more indivisible than that.

There is no greater security than being in Christ and being indwelt by Him. That position of safety continues as long as Christ continues; that is, forever.

8
Members of the Body

The moment a person trusts the Lord Jesus, the Holy Spirit places him in the body of Christ. That is another name for the Church. Christ is the Head and all believers are members. Paul writes, "For as the body is one and has many members, but all the members of that one body, being many, are one body, so also is Christ (1 Cor. 12:12). Here is an unprecedented use of the name "Christ." It refers not only to the Head in heaven, but also to the members in heaven and on earth. This speaks eloquently of the oneness that exists between the Lord and His own.

In the chapter cited, the apostle draws an analogy between the members of the human body and those of the body of Christ. He emphasizes that no member is unimportant: each one is essential and has a unique role to fill. And no member should feel self-sufficient: they are all dependent on one another.

Now suppose the inconceivable should happen! A member removes himself from the body by an act of his own will. He decides that he doesn't want to be a member any longer. This is indeed strange! It was an act of divine power that joined him to the body, but now he is able to undo that by his own power. Impossible!

Or suppose, as some believe, that the Lord removes a believer from the body because of serious and prolonged sin. This is not the way the Church's Head is portrayed in Ephesians 5. There He is the Savior of the body, not the Destroyer (v. 23). He loves the Church and gave Himself for it (v. 25). He doesn't hate His own flesh, but nourishes and cherishes it (v. 29).

The perfections of the Lord Jesus forbid that His body should ever be incomplete, mutilated, or have amputated members. His

37

eventual purpose is to have a glorious Church without spot, wrinkle, or blemish, or any such thing. This certainly bars any imperfection or missing members.

Harold Barker points out that because we are members of Christ's body, our destiny is linked with His destiny. Where He is for eternity, there we will be also (Jn. 14:3).[1]

ENDNOTE

1   Barker, Harold P., *Secure Forever,* Neptune, NJ: Loizeaux Brothers, 1974, p. 78.

9
Eternal Life or Non-Eternal?

One of the most loved verses in the Bible is John 3:16:

For God so loved the world that He gave His only begotten Son, that whoever believes in Him should not perish but have everlasting life.

Millions have rested their eternal destiny on this unbreakable promise of God that if they believe on His unique Son, they will have everlasting life.

John 3:15 says essentially the same thing:

...That whoever believes in Him should not perish but have eternal life.

Anyone who believes in Christ is assured that he will never perish, but will have as a present possession a life that is eternal.

Belief and everlasting life are linked again in John 3:36:

He who believes in the Son has everlasting life; and he who does not believe the Son shall not see life, but the wrath of God abides on him.

Whether a person sees life or suffers the eternal wrath of God depends on whether he or she believes in the Son of God.

Whoever drinks of this water will thirst again, but whoever drinks of the water that I shall give him will never thirst. But the water that I shall give him will become in him a fountain of water springing up into everlasting life (Jn. 4:13-14).

The water that the world offers does not give lasting satisfaction.

Jesus gives the good news of salvation through faith in Him. Whoever drinks of this water, that is, whoever believes on Him, will never thirst again. He receives a life that will never end. He will never need to thirst for it again because he has it eternally. He will have an inner spring gushing up to eternal life.

The promise of eternal life is unmistakably clear in John 5:24:

Most assuredly, I say to you, he who hears My word and believes in Him who sent Me has everlasting life, and shall not come into judgment, but has passed from death into life.

Here He prefaces the promise with "most assuredly,"[1] as if to drive home the certainty of His words. The one who believes on Him already has everlasting life. And as if to guard against any misunderstanding, the Savior adds, "shall not come into condemnation." And if that is not enough, He adds, "has passed from death into life."

The Lord Jesus could hardly have said it more clearly and strongly than He did in John 6:47:

Most assuredly, I say to you, he who believes in Me has everlasting life.

Anyone who believes in Him has life that is eternal. Notice there is not a single condition or exception.

Now I submit that the ordinary person reading these verses would get the distinct impression that eternal life is the present possession of all those who believe in the Lord Jesus Christ. Cream lies on the surface. The clear meaning on the surface is that faith and salvation are joined inseparably. Those who believe are saved eternally.

Well, how then do some people deny this, and teach that the believer's security is conditional?

First of all, they have a rather involved way of contending that eternal life is not necessarily eternal. They are correct when they point out that eternal life denotes not only duration but a quality of life. It is more than endless *existence*, because even the unsaved will exist eternally. It is a kind of life—the life of Christ that is imparted to a believer at the time of his conversion. No unsaved person has it.

But then they seem to disregard the duration aspect of this life and go on to say that you have this quality of life only as long as you continue to walk in obedience to the commandments of the Lord. In other words, the permanence of this life is only at the moment of speaking. You may have it now, but you could forfeit it within the next hour. If that were true, then the word should be "temporary" or "conditional."

We are not allowed to separate the quality of eternal life from its duration. If I receive the life of Christ by faith, I have it eternally because that's what it is—eternal life. Our Lord didn't say, "Believe on Me and you will have conditional life." He said, "eternal life." And that's exactly what He meant.

To know Christ is eternal life (Jn. 17:3). Once a person knows Christ, it is impossible for to decide not to know Him any longer.

The word *eternal* means unending. It is used of God (1 Tim. 1:17) and of the Holy Spirit (Heb. 9:14). The judgment of the unsaved is eternal (Mk. 3:29; Heb. 6:2), as are also the fires of hell (Jude 1:7). The redemption Christ purchased for us is eternal (Heb. 9:12), and the life of the believer is eternal (Jn. 6:47). In none of the verses that contain the words "eternal life" is it ever hinted that the life can be forfeited by sin.

In two verses, the apostle Paul speaks of eternal life as a hope:

In hope of eternal life which God, who cannot lie, promised before time began (Titus 1:2).

That having been justified by His grace we should become heirs according to the hope of eternal life (Titus 3:7).

This might create the impression that we can't be sure of it until life on earth ends. When we use the word *hope* today, there is usually an element of doubt. We cherish a desire but without any definite assurance that it will be fulfilled.

But as already pointed out, that is not the case with *hope* in the

New Testament. There it describes a certainty, because it is based on the promise of God. Nothing in the universe is more sure than that. We already possess eternal life, but the hope of it is the glorified state in heaven.

The Christian hope cannot disappoint us:

Now hope does not disappoint, because the love of God has been poured out in our hearts by the Holy Spirit who was given to us (Rom. 5:5).

This hope we have as an anchor of the soul, both sure and steadfast, and which enters the Presence behind the veil, where the forerunner has entered for us, even Jesus, having become High Priest forever according to the order of Melchizedek (Heb. 6:19-20).

The Lord Jesus, our forerunner, has already entered heaven, which is here described as "the Presence behind the veil." If He has entered **for us,** what can it mean but that we will follow Him there?

But there is another way in which the advocates of conditional salvation seek to advance their cause. In addition to redefining the word "eternal," they seek to show from Greek grammar that the present tense of the verb "believe" always means a continuous process, not a single act of faith. In other words, you must believe and keep on believing.[2] Stop believing and you are no longer saved.

Those who say this are relying on an overly simplistic approach to grammar. The kind of verb tense used for "believe" in the verses above does not carry any implications about the type of action involved.[3] It does not always describe continuous action. It may refer to a single act. For example, "He who comes down from heaven" (Jn. 6:33) describes the incarnation. It was a single act, not constantly repeated. The same tense is used in such expressions as "Blessed are the dead who die in the Lord" (Rev. 14:13), which certainly cannot mean "...who die and go on dying"!

In John 3:14-15, Jesus used the picture of the brazen serpent in the wilderness (Num. 21:6-9). When the Israelites had been bitten by poisonous snakes, God commanded Moses to put a brass serpent on a pole and lift it up. Whenever a dying person looked at the serpent, he would recover. He did not have to gaze and keep on gazing. One look was enough. It had permanent results. Just as one look brought physical healing, so one act of saving faith in Christ brings eternal salvation. That is the gist of the teaching in verses 14-15.

Jesus told the woman of Samaria, "Whoever drinks of the water that I shall give him will never thirst" (Jn. 4:14). Did He mean "drinks and keeps on drinking?" Obviously not. If a person has to drink continually, then he does thirst again. The meaning is clear: One drink of the life-giving water quenches one's thirst forever. In this passage, drinking is a synonym for believing. A single act of faith provides a "fountain of water springing up into everlasting life."

When Paul told the Philippian jailer to "believe on the Lord Jesus Christ" (Acts 16:31), he called for a definite, instantaneous action.[4]

Of course, in saying this, we must keep in mind that if a person is truly born again, he will not cease believing.[5] To believe in Christ is as vital a part of his spiritual life as breathing is to his physical. He cannot stop breathing indefinitely by an act of his will. Neither can he stop believing.

To summarize, the consistent testimony of the New Testament is that God gives a life that is eternal to those who believe in the Lord Jesus Christ. There is no suggestion in any of those promises that that life can be forfeited. It is true that there are a few passages that seem to allow for exceptions, but a few cannot contradict a multitude. And those few, when rightly understood, do not at all deny the fact that the believer is eternally secure. We hope to demonstrate this in the pages that follow.

ENDNOTES

1 The literal rendering is "Amen, Amen." This is the Hebrew for "so be it" or "that's the way it's going to be."

2 Advocates of eternal security and those who believe in conditional security appeal to the Greek text of the New Testament to prove their point. But a knowledge of Greek grammar does not settle the matter conclusively. If it did, the case would have been closed long ago. When Greek scholars can't agree, we should not feel disadvantaged in using our English translations.

3 In John 6:47, it is actually a present participle with a definite article, literally "the believing" or "the believing one." It can be and is best taken as a characteristic of the person spoken of. Hence, here: "the believer in Me." It describes a person rather than the duration of his action.

4 The command to believe is in the aorist tense, which here stresses a decisive act, not continuity.

5 It is part of the intercessory work of Christ at the present time to pray His saints home. This is illustrated by the words He spoke to Peter before Peter denied Him with oaths and curses: "I have prayed for you, that your faith fail not." Peter's courage and his testimony would fail, but his faith would not fail because it was sustained by Christ. *ed.*

10
Ability or Performance?

There are marvelous scriptures that assure us that God is able to save and keep us to the end. But those who believe in probational salvation would rob them of their preciousness by saying that just because He is *able* to do something doesn't mean He *will* do it. Just because He is able to aid those who are tempted (Heb. 2:18) doesn't guarantee that He will do it. The fact that He is able to subdue all things to Himself (Phil. 3:21) doesn't mean that it will ever happen.

Not to worry! For every verse that speaks of His ability to save or to keep eternally, there are others that make performance certain.

In 2 Timothy 1:12, Paul expressed the conviction that the Lord was able to keep what he had committed to Him until that Day. He was able—but would He do it? Definitely yes! The apostle had no doubt. He said, "The Lord will deliver me from every evil work and preserve me for His heavenly kingdom" (2 Tim. 4:18).

The writer to the Hebrews exulted: "He is able to save to the uttermost those who come to God through Him, since He always lives to make intercession for them" (7:25). His present ministry of pleading our cause guarantees that His ability will be converted to accomplishment. But, if that isn't enough, there is the added pledge of divine honor that "He who has begun a good work in you will perform it until the day of Jesus Christ" (Phil. 1:6).

> *The work which His goodness began,*
> *The arm of His strength will complete.*
> *His promise is Yea and Amen,*
> *And never was forfeited yet.*
> *Things future, nor things that are now,*

45

> *Not all things below or above,*
> *Can make Him His purpose forego,*
> *Or sever my soul from His love.*
> —Augustus M. Toplady

Conditional salvationists raise a somewhat similar argument concerning verses like John 6:39-40:

> *This is the will of the Father who sent Me, that of all He has given Me I should lose nothing, but should raise it up at the last day. And this is the will of Him who sent Me, that everyone who sees the Son and believes in Him may have everlasting life; and I will raise him up at the last day.*

They say, "Oh, yes, God's will is that none of those whom He gives to the Son should be lost, but that doesn't mean that all will be saved. God does not will that any should perish (2 Pet. 3:9), but we know that many *do* perish."

The argument is faulty. It is God's will that the Son should lose none of those whom the Father has given him. It is God's will that the Lord Jesus should raise them all up on the last day.

The Son always does the Father's will (Jn. 8:29). Whatever the Father charges the Son to do will be done. This means that none of those whom God gave to Christ will be lost. They will all see Him, will believe in Him, will have everlasting life, and will be raised up at the last day.

Our God and Savior is able to keep us from stumbling, and to present us faultless before the presence of His glory with exceeding joy (Jude 1:24). But does that mean He *will* do it? Paul sets our minds at rest with the assurance that Jesus Christ "will confirm you to the end, that you may be blameless in the day of our Lord Jesus Christ" (1 Cor. 1:8).

Our glorious Lord is able to keep, save, subdue, and aid those who are tempted. And in all these cases His ability is equivalent to His performance. The fact that He is able includes the promise that He will *do* it.

11
Assurance or Uncertainty?

The vast majority of New Testament Scriptures give all those who have ever been *genuinely* born again full assurance that they will reach heaven at last. It is clearly the design of the Holy Scriptures to give God's children complete confidence that once they have received God's gift of salvation through faith in Christ, they are sure of reaching the Father's house.

There are, first of all, the many unfailing promises that whoever receives Jesus Christ as Lord and Savior by a definite act of faith is saved, regenerated, justified, and reconciled. He or she will never be condemned but has passed from death to life.

But then there are many passages where the Lord Jesus or the apostles spoke with certainty about the future of believers. For example, in the story of the lost sheep, the Savior said, "There is joy in the presence of the angels of God over one sinner who repents" (Lk. 15:10). As soon as a sinner repents, all heaven explodes in rejoicing. The celebration is not postponed until the angels find out if the saved one fulfills certain conditions! If his eternal life depends on something he must do, then the ecstasy would be premature.

In another place, the Savior guaranteed His disciples that He was going to prepare a place for them in the Father's house and that they would be with Him there (Jn. 14:3). He said, "Because I live you will live also" (Jn. 14:19)—a clear promise of their future blessedness. These promises were not conditional on their accomplishments.

There was no doubt in the apostle Paul's mind that in his eternal home, that is, heaven, he would know as he was known (1 Cor. 13:12). He knew that he and the Corinthian believers would all be changed, that is, they would receive glorified bodies (1 Cor. 15:51-52). Speaking for all the redeemed, he said, "We know that if our earthly house, this tent, is destroyed, we have a building from God, a house not made with hands, eternal in the heavens" (2 Cor. 5:1). Without any conditions attached, he expressed utter confidence that when they would be absent from the body, they would be present with the Lord (2 Cor. 5:8). No restrictions are added to any of these assurances.

He expressed confidence that even the spirit of a Corinthian believer who had committed incest would "be saved in the day of the Lord Jesus" (1 Cor. 5:5), even though he would suffer discipline in the meantime.

Writing to the Philippians, he said that for him to die was gain (Phil. 1:21), and there was no suggestion that this was conditional on his faithful performance. He cheered them with the certainty that the Lord Jesus would transform their lowly bodies so that they would be conformed to His glorious body (Phil. 3:21), but he didn't add, "if you endure to the end."

How could he promise the Colossians that they would appear with Christ in glory (Col. 3:4) if they must always obey the commandments of the Lord to be sure? How would he have known?

Paul obviously believed in eternal security. He expected to be in heaven, and he expected the Thessalonians to be there too, because he said to them, "What is our hope, our joy, our crown of rejoicing? Is it not even you in the presence of our Lord Jesus Christ at His coming?" (1 Thess. 2:19). He didn't say, "But you and I must keep on believing," because he knew that they would. Looking forward to the coming of Christ for the Church, he said, "And thus we shall always be with the Lord" (1 Thess. 4:17b). Again in 2 Thessalonians 1:7, he assures the saints of unconditional rest when the Lord Jesus is revealed from heaven with His mighty angels.

Toward the end of his life, when it was still possible for him to fail, he said, "I have fought the good fight, I have finished the race, I have kept the faith. Finally, there is laid up for me the crown of righteousness, which the Lord, the righteous Judge, will give to me on that Day, and not to me only but also to all who have loved His appearing" (2 Tim. 4:7-8). He didn't trust his own strength, but knew that the Lord would preserve him for His heavenly kingdom (2 Tim. 4:18).

Peter, too, believed in eternal security. He wrote of the grace that would be brought to his readers at the revelation of Jesus Christ (1 Pet. 1:13). The word "if" is not any part of the sentence. He knew that when Christ's glory was revealed, the suffering believers would be glad with exceeding joy (1 Pet. 4:13). How could he have known this if their eventual salvation depended in any way on their attainments? He and his readers looked for new heavens and a new earth in which righteousness dwells (2 Pet. 3:13). He could not say this if he believed in conditional salvation.

Finally, the apostle John gives his readers the unspeakable assurance, "...we know that when He is revealed, we shall be like Him, for we shall see Him as He is" (1 Jn. 3:2b). It is an unqualified certainty for every child of God.

It's no wonder that God's people down through the centuries have rested their assurance of heaven on the work of Christ alone and not on any unpredictable and dubious achievements of their own.

It's only when salvation is by grace through faith and apart from works of any kind that a person can be assured of eternal security. The moment you add legal conditions to be fulfilled by the believer, assurance is impossible, because you can't know if he or she will fulfill the conditions properly.

12
Apostates or Backsliders?
Part 1

Those who contend for conditional salvation base their case on the book of Hebrews more than any other book in the Bible. Before examining the individual passages which they cite, let's take a bird's eye view of the epistle itself.

In the early days of the Church, the gospel went out to the Jewish people first. Many of them were genuinely converted to the Christian faith. Others were attracted to the light of the gospel and became nominal adherents. Some of these went so far as to be baptized and to become members of a Christian assembly, thus identifying themselves with the Christian community.

For the Jews, it was an act of treason to profess to become a Christian. Those who did so were denounced as renegades and turncoats. They were subject to excommunication, ostracism, disinheritance, and even physical abuse. Their religious leaders, families, and friends put them under enormous pressure to return to the elaborate ceremonial system of Judaism. They reminded these uncertain seekers of what they were abandoning:

- the glories of the Old Testament prophets.
- the ministry of angels in the history of the nation.
- the leadership of Moses and Joshua.
- the priesthood of Aaron, and the sacrificial system.

The choice was clear. Either go on to full-fledged trust in Christ as Lord and Savior or willfully repudiate Him. To fall away was to commit the sin of apostasy, for which there is no repentance.

This then is the situation which the writer to the Hebrews faced. At times he is urging true believers to lives of faith and endurance.

But for the most part he is warning Jews who were straddling the fence against the sin of apostasy. He shows that Christ is the fulfillment of all the types and shadows in Judaism.

The word *apostate* comes from a Greek word meaning "one who stands off or defects."[1] First of all, it describes a person who professes to be a Christian but who has never received Christ by a definite act of faith. The apostle John had apostates in mind when he wrote: "They went out from us, but they were not of us; for if they had been of us, they would have continued with us; but they went out that they might be made manifest, that none of them were of us" (1 Jn. 2:19). It was not a case of leaving one Christian assembly for another. Rather it was an utter rejection of the Christian faith. Their departure showed that they were "not of us," that is, that they were not true believers. If they had been, they would have continued in the faith, because true faith always has the quality of continuance. In departing, they showed that they were not true members of the Christian community. Their association with it was superficial.

It should be clear that there is a big difference between *backsliding* and *apostasy*. A Christian can fall but he can't fall away. His fellowship with God can be broken but not his relationship. An apostate has never had a true relationship with God. When a believer sins, sooner or later he blames himself and confesses his sin; the apostate falls into sin and moral failure and blames God. The backslider repents and is forgiven; the apostate doesn't worry about his sin. In fact, he is often defiant about it. He finds no forgiveness.[2] Peter was a backslider; Judas was an apostate. "Peter went out and wept bitterly" (Lk. 22:62), but afterward returned to his Master (Jn. 21:15-19). Judas went out and hanged himself (Mt. 27:5).

Notice the seriousness of the sin of apostasy. It is equivalent to crucifying again the Son of God for oneself and putting Him to an open shame (Heb. 6:6). It is the same as trampling the Son of God underfoot, counting His blood a common thing, and insulting the Holy Spirit (Heb. 10:29). Apostates are antichrists (1 Jn. 2:18).

Now let's examine the passages in Hebrews that are commonly used to support conditional security or to disprove eternal security.

Therefore we must give the more earnest heed to the things we have heard, lest we drift away. For if the word spoken through angels proved steadfast, and every transgression and disobedience received a just reward, how shall we escape if we neglect so great a salvation, which at the first began to be spoken by the Lord, and was confirmed to us by those who heard Him? (Heb. 2:1-3)

This passage is a warning against apostasy. The readers are reminded that the penalty for breaking the Ten Commandments was death. If that was so, a much greater doom awaits those who neglect the gospel. Here neglect means to disregard, to slight, or to ignore.

We must not be confused by the use of *we* here, as if the writer included himself and other true believers. Not so. They had already accepted the gospel. This is the editorial use of *we*; the Bible authors had as much right to use it as we do. Here it means those who were in danger of neglecting the gospel.

These are not good verses to prove that a believer may eventually spend eternity in hell.

6...but Christ as a Son over His own house, whose house we are if we hold fast the confidence and the rejoicing of the hope firm to the end. 7 Therefore, as the Holy Spirit says: "Today, if you will hear His voice, 8 do not harden your hearts as in the rebellion, In the day of trial in the wilderness, 9 where your fathers tested Me, tried Me, And saw My works forty years. 10 Therefore I was angry with that generation, and said, 'They always go astray in their heart, And they have not known My ways.' 11 So I swore in My wrath, 'They shall not enter My rest.'" 12 Beware, brethren, lest there be in any of you an evil heart of unbelief in departing from the living God; 13 but exhort one another daily, while it is called "Today," lest any of you be hardened through the deceitfulness of sin. 14 For we have become partakers of Christ if we hold the beginning of our confidence steadfast to the end, 15 while it is said: "Today, if you will hear His voice, Do not harden your hearts as in the rebellion." 16 For who, having

*heard, rebelled? Indeed, was it not all who came out of Egypt,
led by Moses? 17 Now with whom was He angry forty years?
Was it not with those who sinned, whose corpses fell in the
wilderness? 18 And to whom did He swear that they would not
enter His rest, but to those who did not obey? 19 So we see that
they could not enter in because of unbelief (Heb. 3:6-19).*

In approaching these verses, remember that the one who wrote
them is addressing a mixed audience. Just as today, some were genuine believers and others had an outward form of godliness but
without the power. The lines were not clearly drawn. No one could
discern in every case whether the person was actually in Christ.
Therefore, it was necessary to warn the undecided against the peril
of apostasy and to assure the others in their faith.

Verse 6. Those who have been born again by faith in the Lord
demonstrate the reality of their faith by holding fast the confidence
and rejoicing of the hope firm to the end. They are not *saved* by
holding fast; that would be salvation by works. It would be a personal attainment of which they could boast. But boasting is exclud-
ed by the principle of faith (Rom. 3:27).

Verses 7-11. Nominal believers should be warned by the experience of Israel in the wilderness. For 40 years, the people provoked
God by their unbelief. Finally, He swore in His wrath that they
would not enter His rest, that is, rest in the land of Canaan.

Verses 12-14. The "brethren" addressed in verse 12 could be
brothers of a common humanity, brethren of the same Jewish nation, or Christian brothers by name only. To depart from the living
God is tantamount to apostatizing. In spite of their profession, they
have become members of Christ only if they hold the beginning of
their confidence steadfast to the end. Once again "holding...stead-
fast" is not the root of salvation; it is the fruit.

Verses 15-19. Faith is the crucial matter. Just as unbelief kept the
Israelites out of God's Canaan rest, so it will keep people out of
God's rest today, as we will see in the next section.

1 *Therefore, since a promise remains of entering His rest, let us*

fear lest any of you seem to have come short of it. 2 For indeed the gospel was preached to us as well as to them; but the word which they heard did not profit them, not being mixed with faith in those who heard it. 3 For we who have believed do enter that rest, as He has said: "So I swore in My wrath, 'They shall not enter My rest,'" although the works were finished from the foundation of the world. 4 For He has spoken in a certain place of the seventh day in this way: "And God rested on the seventh day from all His works"; 5 and again in this place: "They shall not enter My rest." 6 Since therefore it remains that some must enter it, and those to whom it was first preached did not enter because of disobedience, 7 again He designates a certain day, saying in David, "Today," after such a long time, as it has been said: "Today, if you will hear His voice, Do not harden your hearts." 8 For if Joshua had given them rest, then He would not afterward have spoken of another day. 9 There remains therefore a rest for the people of God. 10 For he who has entered His rest has himself also ceased from his works as God did from His. 11 Let us therefore be diligent to enter that rest, lest anyone fall according to the same example of disobedience. 12 For the word of God is living and powerful, and sharper than any two-edged sword, piercing even to the division of soul and spirit, and of joints and marrow, and is a discerner of the thoughts and intents of the heart. 13 And there is no creature hidden from His sight, but all things are naked and open to the eyes of Him to whom we must give account. 14 Seeing then that we have a great High Priest who has passed through the heavens, Jesus the Son of God, let us hold fast our confession. 15 For we do not have a High Priest who cannot sympathize with our weaknesses, but was in all points tempted as we are, yet without sin. 16 Let us therefore come boldly to the throne of grace, that we may obtain mercy and find grace to help in time of need (Heb. 4:1-16).

Four rests are mentioned in Hebrews: God's creation rest (4:4); Israel's rest in Canaan (3:11); the present rest of faith (4:1, 3a, 8-

10); its full fruition, the eternal Sabbath rest yet to come (4:9).

Although the flow of thought is admittedly difficult, the argument seems to be this: God's promise of rest was not fulfilled by His creation rest. And Joshua did not lead the people into that rest, because later God was still speaking about it in the time of David. Those who believe in Christ enter that rest (v. 3a). They have ceased trying to earn their salvation by their own works, and now enjoy rest of conscience, knowing that the Savior finished the work on the cross. The heavenly rest awaits all God's people.

Nominal Christians (and all unbelievers) should be careful not to come short of the promised rest, but be diligent to enter it by putting their faith in the Lord Jesus. Unbelief never goes undetected, because the Living Word is omniscient.

And since true believers are also accountable to Him, they should hold fast their confession. However, they can't do this in their own strength, but through their High Priest who gives grace to help in time of need.

Apparently those who hold the falling away doctrine point to verses 1, 11, and 14 to support their position that true believers may eventually be lost. They fail to see that verses 1 and 11 are for those who have not as yet come to true faith in the Lord Jesus. They do not enjoy rest of conscience. And since they have come short of it, they are in danger of falling into the snare of apostasy. Verse 14 is an encouragement to believers to be valiant in their confession of Christ, assured that their High Priest will grant them all needed strength.

Though He was a Son, yet He learned obedience by the things which He suffered. And having been perfected, He became the author of eternal salvation to all who obey Him (Heb. 5:8-9).

The proof text used by Arminians here is verse 9: Christ is the author of eternal salvation to those who obey Him. The implication is that if you cease to obey Him, you forfeit your salvation. But this sounds precariously like salvation by works!

We must understand that the gospel is a message to be obeyed, and you obey it by believing on the Lord Jesus Christ. In this context, obedience is a synonym for faith. That is what Paul elsewhere speaks of as the obedience of faith (Rom. 1:5; 16:26). And Luke speaks of a great many priests who were obedient to the faith (Acts 6:7). Their salvation experience was a single event, not a process.

One of the passages that is most frequently used to show that a true believer can eventually be lost is Hebrews 6:4-8.

> *For it is impossible for those who were once enlightened, and have tasted of the heavenly gift, and have become partakers of the Holy Spirit, and have tasted the good word of God and the powers of the age to come, if they fall away, to renew them again to repentance, since they crucify again for themselves the Son of God, and put Him to an open shame. For the earth which drinks in the rain that often comes upon it, and bears herbs useful for those by whom it is cultivated, receives blessing from God; but if it bears thorns and briers, it is rejected and near to being cursed, whose end is to be burned.*

In fairness, it must be admitted that there are many different interpretations of these verses. Even among those who believe in eternal security, there are various views.[3] Therefore, we must adopt the one that we think best fits into the context and that agrees with the rest of the inspired Word. To the writer, this controversial passage is dealing with apostates.

They were once enlightened. There should be no question that this can be true of unconverted people. It's all too possible to be enlightened without responding to the light.

They have tasted of the heavenly gift. The heavenly gift may refer to either the Lord Jesus or the Holy Spirit. The word "taste" may mean savor without swallowing, as in Matthew 27:34; when Jesus had tasted the sour wine mingled with gall, He would not drink. Or it may mean to become acquainted with something by experience. For example, Jesus, by the grace of God, tasted death for everyone. There it was death to the fullest. So the word here in Hebrews is not decisive in itself. But it's enough to say that a person may be acquainted with the heavenly gift without accepting Him.

They have become partakers of the Holy Spirit. Notice that it does not say they have been indwelt, baptized, or filled by the Holy Spirit. But they had partaken of such ministries of the Holy Spirit as conviction of sin and the knowledge of the way of salvation.

They have tasted the good Word of God. It goes without saying that it is possible to hear the Word without believing it. There are people who have heads full of Bible knowledge who die in their sins. Tasting is not enough.

They have tasted the powers of the age to come. The Hebrews described here had witnessed the miracles that accompanied the preaching of the gospel by the apostles. These miracles are described as "the powers of the age to come." This means that they will be repeated in the Millennium when the Lord Jesus reigns as King of kings and Lord of lords.

Bearing in mind, then, that these five characteristics can be true of unbelievers, let's consider the rest of the passage.

If the people described fall away, it is impossible to renew them to repentance. They may have repented once in a superficial way (2 Cor. 7:10) without believing on Christ, but once they apostatize, their doom is sealed. They have passed beyond redemption point. This is borne out by history. No real apostate has ever come to a saving knowledge of the Lord Jesus.

If this passage were talking about true believers who lapsed into sin, it would mean that they could *never* be saved again. But that proves too much for those who hold the falling away doctrine.

These people are not genuine children of God because "they crucify again for themselves the Son of God, and put Him to an open shame." That is scarcely the behavior that characterizes those who have been born of God.

In verse 7, the writer likens true believers to well-watered land that yields a suitable harvest blessed by God. Apostates are like land that "bears thorns and thistles," which is "rejected and near to being cursed, whose end is to be burned." The expression "near to being cursed" does not offer some other possibility. Rather it expresses the certainty of judgment, and this is confirmed by the verdict "whose end is to be burned."

So that no doubt remains concerning the spiritual condition of the apostates he has been describing, the writer adds the deciding affirmative in verse 9, "But, beloved, we are confident of better things concerning you, yes, things that accompany salvation." Here he addresses genuine Christians as "beloved." He is persuaded that they do not produce thorns and briers, that they are not near to being cursed, and that their end is not to be burned. He is persuaded that they are characterized by the things that accompany salvation, which is not true of those described in the preceding verses.

9 *But, beloved, we are confident of better things concerning you, yes, things that accompany salvation, though we speak in this manner.* 10 *For God is not unjust to forget your work and labor of love which you have shown toward His name, in that you have ministered to the saints, and do minister.* 11 *And we desire that each one of you show the same diligence to the full assurance of hope until the end,* 12 *that you do not become sluggish, but imitate those who through faith and patience inherit the promises.* 13 *For when God made a promise to Abraham, because He could swear by no one greater, He swore by Himself,* 14 *saying, "Surely blessing I will bless you, and multiplying I will multiply you."* 15 *And so, after he had patiently endured, he obtained the promise.* 16 *For men indeed swear by the greater, and an oath for confirmation is for them an end of all dispute.* 17 *Thus God, determining to show more abundantly to the heirs of promise the immutability of His counsel, confirmed it by an oath,* 18 *that by two immutable things, in which it is impossible for God to lie, we might have strong consolation, who have fled for refuge to lay hold of the hope set before us.* 19 *This hope we have as an anchor of the soul, both sure and steadfast, and which enters the Presence behind the veil,* 20 *where the forerunner has entered for us, even Jesus, having become High Priest forever according to the order of Melchizedek* (Heb. 6:9-20).

Here we have a strong paragraph on the eternal security of the believer. Strangely enough, it is enlisted to prove the exact opposite! It's addressed to those who were decided Christians. As we have seen, verse 9 says they were characterized by the things that accompany salvation. The next verse adds further evidence of the reality of their faith. They are then encouraged to continue in their diligent ministry to the saints, and not to become sluggish. They should imitate those who through faith and patience inherit [the fulfillment of] the promises. The verses that follow clearly demonstrate that faith and patience are not the *means* by which they inherit [the fulfillment of] the promises but their spiritual *attitude* on the way to the goal.

God made an unconditional promise to Abraham to bless him and to multiply his offspring. Since God cannot lie, this promise was as certain as if it had already been fulfilled. It did not depend one iota on Abraham's performance. Nothing could hinder it from coming to pass because everything depended on God. Abraham patiently waited for the fulfillment.

God has made an unconditional covenant of grace, promising eternal salvation to all who repent of their sins and receive Christ as Lord and Savior by faith.[4] Since God cannot lie, the promise is absolutely sure of fulfillment. A believer is as certain of heaven as if he was already there. The saints in heaven are "more happy but not more secure" than we are. The strength of the covenant is that everything depends on God.

Verses 18-20 give four pictures to stress the believer's security:

The first is a city of refuge to which we flee to lay hold of the hope set before us. Christ is the city of refuge, and the hope is eternal salvation. Because this hope is based on God's work, there can be no element of doubt or uncertainty.

The second figure is an anchor. Our anchor, the hope of everlasting glory, is cast in the presence of God where nothing can move it. It is steadfast and sure.

That is not all. Jesus Himself has gone inside the veil as our Forerunner. His presence there is our guarantee that we too will reach heaven at last.

Finally, He is there as our High Priest. His life for us there guarantees our eternal preservation (Rom. 5:10). He lives forever to make intercession for us (Heb. 7:25).

Another passage that describes an apostate is in chapter 10, verses 26-31.

For if we sin willfully after we have received the knowledge of the truth, there no longer remains a sacrifice for sins, but a certain fearful expectation of judgment, and fiery indignation which will devour the adversaries. Anyone who has rejected Moses' law dies without mercy on the testimony of two or three witnesses. Of how much worse punishment, do you suppose, will he be thought worthy who has trampled the Son of God underfoot, counted the blood of the covenant by which he was sanctified a common thing, and insulted the Spirit of grace? For we know Him who said, "Vengeance is Mine, I will repay," says the Lord. And again, "The Lord will judge His people." It is a fearful thing to fall into the hands of the living God.

The willful sin in verse 26 is apostasy. It is true that, in one sense, nearly all sin is willful, but this one is willful in a way that is not true of any other, as we shall see.

When an apostate renounces Christ after receiving the knowledge of the truth, he has forever cut himself off from the cleansing virtue of Christ's finished sacrifice for sins. He has taken his place with the enemies of Christ and thus shares their doom. Receiving the knowledge of the truth is not enough. It must be followed by receiving Christ.

If it was a capital offense to reject the law of Moses, it is far more serious to commit the sin of apostasy, because it means to:

a. trample under foot the Son of God, picturing scorn and contempt;

b. count the blood of the covenant by which he was sanctified a common thing;

c. insult the Spirit of grace.

Let us look at these monstrous offenses one by one, and then ask ourselves if they paint an accurate picture of a real child of God.

There have been times in the history of the Church when people who wanted to repudiate Christ and return to their ancestral religion were required to pass a symbolic test. The blood of an animal was spilt on the floor. Then they were told, "This blood represents the blood of Christ. Now walk over it." If they did, they escaped persecution in this life—but lost their souls in the next. This is true of any who abandon a professed faith in Christ.

An apostate counts the blood of Christ of no more value than that of an unclean animal. Yet it is the blood of the covenant by which he is sanctified. By becoming a nominal Christian, he is sanctified, that is, set apart in a position of external privilege, just as an unbelieving husband is sanctified by a believing wife (1 Cor. 7:14). To be sanctified does not necessarily mean to be saved.

To turn away from the sole and sufficient Savior is the same as insulting the Spirit of grace. It is to look with scorn on the Holy Spirit and His ministry of exalting Christ as the only way to God the Father.

Again the description of an apostate is followed by a description of the righteous punishment of God that awaits him or her. The sentence "The Lord shall judge His people" might create the impression that the writer is speaking about true believers. But not so. All men and women are God's people by creation (Acts 17:28). The nation of Israel was God's ancient earthly people (Deut. 14:2). At the present time all who believe in His Son are His chosen people (1 Pet. 2:9). But when it says, "The Lord shall judge His people," it can't mean true believers, because the Savior Himself promised that those who hear His word and believe on the One who sent Him "will not come into judgment" (Jn. 5:24). The author quotes Deuteronomy 32:36 (or Ps. 135:14) in the context of apostates, not true believers. The clause "the Lord will judge His people" confirms the previous quotation, "Vengeance is Mine; I will repay, says the Lord."

A Christian can backslide. He can get out of fellowship with the

Lord. He can commit any sin against which he is warned in the Scriptures. But he cannot maliciously renounce Christ. He may fall seven times but he will rise again (Prov. 24:16).

But recall the former days in which, after you were illuminated, you endured a great struggle with sufferings: partly while you were made a spectacle both by reproaches and tribulations, and partly while you became companions of those who were so treated; for you had compassion on me in my chains, and joyfully accepted the plundering of your goods, knowing that you have a better and an enduring possession for yourselves in heaven. Therefore do not cast away your confidence, which has great reward. For you have need of endurance, so that after you have done the will of God, you may receive the promise: "For yet a little while and He who is coming will come and will not tarry. Now the just shall live by faith; but if anyone draws back, my soul has no pleasure in him." But we are not of those who draw back to perdition, but of those who believe to the saving of the soul (Heb. 10:32-39).

Believing Hebrews are reminded of all they had suffered because of their known faith in the Lord Jesus. They shared the persecutions of other believers, ministered to the writer of the epistle in his imprisonment, and joyfully accepted the loss of their possessions, realizing that their real treasures were in heaven.

They should not lose heart now but should bear up under the trials so that, having done the will of God, they might receive [the fulfillment of] the promise. There is no suggestion in verses 35-36 that the reception of the promise depends on their endurance. Rather this is the way they should live anticipating the Lord's return (v. 37).

The first part of verse 38 describes true believers—"the just shall live by faith." It means "the justified-by-faith ones shall live." The rest of the verse describes an apostate—"if anyone draws back." But draws back from what? From true faith in the Lord Jesus.

Someone will ask, "How do you know it means that?" Because it says so. "We [true believers] are not of those who draw back to perdition [apostates], but of those who believe to the saving of the soul [believers]." In other words, apostates do not believe to the saving of the soul. They profess faith for a while but then they draw back.

These all died in faith, not having received the promises, but having seen them afar off were assured of them, embraced them and confessed that they were strangers and pilgrims on the earth. For those who say such things declare plainly that they seek a homeland. And truly if they had called to mind that country from which they had come out, they would have had opportunity to return. But now they desire a better, that is, a heavenly country. Therefore God is not ashamed to be called their God, for He has prepared a city for them (Heb. 11:13-16).

I confess I was surprised and puzzled to find this listed among passages that are used to support conditional salvation. After further study I could only conclude that verse 15 is the proof text: "they would have had opportunity to return." It is employed to say that just as the patriarchs could have changed their minds about continuing on the route to Canaan, so true believers can stop believing and return to their unsaved lifestyle. It says that the initial act of saving faith is not enough. It must be followed by continued faith. A person can forfeit his salvation by deliberately ceasing to believe.

But that does not fit the facts. I might have the opportunity to return to my unconverted lifestyle, but I do not have the desire or the inclination. If a person says he is a Christian and decides to return to a life of sin, it shows that he never became a new creation in Christ Jesus in the first place.

To suggest that the initial act of faith does not determine final destiny is a perversion of the gospel. It means that Christ did not atone for all a believer's sins, but only for those up to the time of conversion. After that, the believer is on his own. Just think of the implications of this view!

1. It denies that Christ is the sole and sufficient Savior; the believer shares in that work.

2. It denies that Christ's work takes care of the penalty for all a Christian's sins, past, present, and future—even though they were all future when He died.

3. It is a denial of salvation by free grace. It suggests that people can merit salvation by their perseverance in faith.

1 *Therefore we also, since we are surrounded by so great a cloud of witnesses, let us lay aside every weight, and the sin which so easily ensnares us, and let us run with endurance the race that is set before us,* 2 *looking unto Jesus, the author and finisher of our faith, who for the joy that was set before Him endured the cross, despising the shame, and has sat down at the right hand of the throne of God.* 3 *For consider Him who endured such hostility from sinners against Himself, lest you become weary and discouraged in your souls.* 4 *You have not yet resisted to bloodshed, striving against sin.* 5 *And you have forgotten the exhortation which speaks to you as to sons: "My son, do not despise the chastening of the Lord, Nor be discouraged when you are rebuked by Him;* 6 *for whom the Lord loves He chastens, And scourges every son whom He receives." * 7 *If you endure chastening, God deals with you as with sons; for what son is there whom a father does not chasten?* 8 *But if you are without chastening, of which all have become partakers, then you are illegitimate and not sons.* 9 *Furthermore, we have had human fathers who corrected us, and we paid them respect. Shall we not much more readily be in subjection to the Father of spirits and live?* 10 *For they indeed for a few days chastened us as seemed best to them, but He for our profit, that we may be partakers of His holiness.* 11 *Now no chastening seems to be joyful for the present, but painful; nevertheless, afterward it yields the peaceable fruit of righteousness to those who have been trained by it.* 12 *Therefore strengthen the hands which hang down, and the feeble knees,* 13 *and make straight paths for your feet, so that what is lame may not be dislocated, but rather be healed.* 14 *Pursue peace with all people, and holiness, without which no*

one will see the Lord: 15 *looking carefully lest anyone fall short of the grace of God; lest any root of bitterness springing up cause trouble, and by this many become defiled;* 16 *lest there be any fornicator or profane person like Esau, who for one morsel of food sold his birthright.* 17 *For you know that afterward, when he wanted to inherit the blessing, he was rejected, for he found no place for repentance, though he sought it diligently with tears* (Heb. 12:1-17).

Hebrews 11-13 are largely exhortations to faith and endurance. However, exhortations are not necessarily commands with threats attached. When I say to a new convert, "Go on for the Lord," I'm not suggesting that he will be eternally damned if he doesn't. With that in mind, let me summarize this section.

Hebrew Christians who are suffering for their faith should be encouraged by the faith and endurance of the heroes of chapter 11. Specifically they should avoid any tendency to doubt or despair, and should run the Christian race with endurance. They should keep in view Jesus, who shows us how to run from start to finish. He endured the hatred of sinners. He endured the cross. They had not yet gone as far as He, resisting unto blood, that is, actually dying.

And they should not despise the child-training of the Lord.[5] (At this time, it was the sufferings they were enduring for Him.) The Father trains only those who are His. So believers should not despise it or be discouraged by it, but should try to learn what He is teaching by it. It is those whom God does not chasten who are illegitimate, that is, they are not believers at all.

Verses 12-14 are general exhortations to mutual encouragement, to the example of a saintly life, to peace, and to holiness. Perhaps the expression "Pursue...holiness, without which no one will see the Lord" might support the idea of conditional security in the minds of some. It shouldn't.

The moment a person is saved, he is sanctified positionally. God gives him a holy standing because he is in Christ. But then God says, in effect, "Now *be* holy. Let your behavior harmonize with your position." This is known as practical sanctification.

Here in verse 12, it is this second aspect of holiness that is in view. We are to pursue holiness. Note that it is a pursuit, not an accomplishment. We never become perfectly holy until we reach heaven.

All true believers long for greater holiness and pursue it, some to a greater extent than others. But since it is a pursuit, Christians need to be exhorted to seek after ever greater Christ-likeness.

Verses 15-17 are another warning against apostasy. But why is it slipped into a chapter of encouragement to Christians? Because the Hebrew-Christian congregation then was like churches today. It included the genuine and the counterfeit, and the message must take that in view.

Notice five things about apostasy:

1. It is a falling short of the grace of God. So near and yet so far. The apostate is illumined but he does not go so far as to be regenerated.

2. It is a root of bitterness, not content to hold its gall in isolation but determined to spread it to others.

3. It is often associated with immorality. Much apostasy has its roots in moral failure.

4. It is profane, that is, it lacks any affinity or appreciation for spiritual realities.

5. It finds no place for repentance.

See that you do not refuse Him who speaks. For if they did not escape who refused Him who spoke on earth, much more shall we not escape if we turn away from Him who speaks from heaven, whose voice then shook the earth; but now He has promised, saying, "Yet once more I will shake not only the earth, but also heaven." Now this, "Yet once more," indicates the removal of those things that are being shaken, as of things that are made, that the things which cannot be shaken may remain. Therefore, since we are receiving a kingdom which cannot be shaken, let us have grace, by which we may serve God acceptably with reverence and godly fear. For our God is a consuming fire (Heb. 12:25-29).

As we have seen before, the writer paints with a broad brush. He speaks to born-again ones and potential apostates almost in the same breath and without identifying his targets. It's a case of "If the shoe fits, wear it."

Once again he contrasts the peril of refusing God as He gave the law at Mount Sinai with the greater peril of refusing Him as He speaks in the gospel from heaven.

This is not the fancied case of someone who believed and then decided not to believe any longer. It refers to a person who has never truly believed in the first place. The same One who shook the earth at Sinai will shake the created universe so that only spiritual realities, such as the eternal kingdom, will survive. The obligation of believers is to serve God acceptably with reverence and godly fear. Only those who have received God's Son can do this.

How are we to understand the closing words, "for our God is a consuming fire"? It is true in at least two ways. His fire will be the eternal doom of all unbelievers. However, when fire is used in connection with the redeemed, it has to do with their works, not their souls (1 Cor. 3:13, 15).

Do not be carried about with various and strange doctrines. For it is good that the heart be established by grace, not with foods which have not profited those who have been occupied with them. We have an altar from which those who serve the tabernacle have no right to eat. For the bodies of those animals, whose blood is brought into the sanctuary by the high priest for sin, are burned outside the camp. Therefore Jesus also, that He might sanctify the people with His own blood, suffered outside the gate. Therefore let us go forth to Him, outside the camp, bearing His reproach. For here we have no continuing city, but we seek the one to come (Heb. 13:9-14).

This paragraph is one of many that are used to show that the Epistle to the Hebrews was written to believers, the implication being that it was written exclusively to those who belong to Christ. It follows from this premise that the verses addressed to apostates were, *ipso facto,* written to believers, and that therefore apostates are members of Christ who can lose their salvation.

The fallacy of the argument lies in the implied word *exclusively.* No one denies that portions of the letter were written to Hebrews who had been soundly converted. But that doesn't require that those who had nothing but an empty profession could not be included. Second Corinthians was written to "the church of God which is at Corinth, with all the saints who are in all Achaia," yet they were told to examine themselves whether they were in the faith (13:5). Galatians was written largely to the churches of Galatia, yet Paul had doubts about some of them (4:20).

Remember those who rule over you, who have spoken the word of God to you, whose faith follow, considering the outcome of their conduct...Obey those who rule over you, and be submissive, for they watch out for your souls, as those who must give account. Let them do so with joy and not with grief, for that would be unprofitable for you (Heb. 13:7, 17).

Again the argument is that these exhortations were clearly written to true saints of God; since apostates figure so strongly in the epistle, such exhortations prove that apostates were Christians at one time. It follows from this that Christians can lose their faith and be lost.

This reasoning fails to see that Hebrews was not written exclusively to believers. No one denies that many exhortations had saints in view. But many others were addressed to Jews who were Christians outwardly, but were under titanic pressure to go back to Judaism.

If the apostates were authentic Christians who subsequently gave up their faith, then they never could be saved again. But this does not harmonize with the views of conditional salvationists. *They* believe that apostates *can* be restored!

It also overlooks the fact that Hebrews 13 contains a sure promise from God that He will not forsake His people:

> *Let your conduct be without covetousness; be content with such things as you have. For He Himself has said, "I will never leave you nor forsake you." So we may boldly say: "The Lord is my helper; I will not fear. What can man do to me?"* (Heb. 13:5-6).

These verses deal primarily with God's provision for believers' physical needs. In the persecution of those days, many believers were facing the loss of their possessions (10:34). Even for the genuine believers among them, this must surely have provided a strong temptation to jealousy and covetousness. The author encouraged them with this reminder that God would provide for them as long as was necessary for them to fulfill His purpose for them in this life. Note that it does not say, "If you keep yourselves from covetousness, He will not forsake you"; it says, in effect, "He will not forsake you; therefore, keep yourselves from covetousness."

And, as Paul did in Romans 5 and 8, we may certainly argue from the lesser to the greater here. God provides even for the physical preservation of His people; shall He then leave their spiritual preservation to their own strength?

It has often been pointed out that in the original, the verse says, "I will never, never, never leave you or forsake you." Emphatic, isn't it![6]

In opposing eternal security, one advocate of the falling away doctrine went so far as to question whether pastors who believe in unconditional security can properly care for the souls of their flock. This is, of course, a subjective judgment that could just as well be used by his opponents.

ENDNOTES

1   The prefix *apo* means "from" or "away," and the rest of the word is from the verb "to stand," hence, to take a stand against what one previously held.

2   Judas was remorseful but it was only regret, not godly repentance (Mt. 27:3; 2 Cor. 7:10). He was a devil (Jn. 6:70). He had never had the bath of regeneration (Jn. 13:10-11). He went to his own place (Acts 1:25). When Jesus called him the son of perdition (Jn. 17:12), the meaning of the verse is this: "Those that You have given Me I have kept, and none of them is lost, but the son of perdition is lost, that the Scripture might be fulfilled." John 18:9 makes it clear that "those whom You gave Me" refers to the Eleven, the true believers, but not to Judas.

3   Some alternative views of those who believe that the passage speaks of true Christians who *cannot* lose their salvation:

• Believers who fall into sin, then want to be renewed unto repentance, that is, saved again. By doing this, they would be putting Christ back on the cross, declaring shamefully that His once-for-all work was not enough to save them once-for-all.
• Christians who commit sin and are subject to God's judgment in this life, though saved eternally.
• Christians who are warned against apostasy and thus effectively prevented from doing it. This is a purely hypothetical interpretation.

An alternative view of those who believe that the passage speaks of true Christians who *can* lose their salvation:

• Believers who are eternally secure unless they commit the one sin of apostasy. *ed.*

4   Repentance and faith are not meritorious works by which we contribute something to Christ's finished work.

5   The word *chastening* includes all that is involved in raising a child—instruction, encouragement, correction, punishment, etc.

6   It is actually a *quintuple* negative in Greek!

13
Apostates or Backsliders?
Part 2

Before leaving the subject of apostasy, it remains for us to examine pertinent passages in 1 John and Jude. They help us in confirming our definition of an apostate and strengthen the case for eternal security.

18 *Little children, it is the last hour; and as you have heard that the Antichrist is coming, even now many antichrists have come, by which we know that it is the last hour. 19 They went out from us, but they were not of us; for if they had been of us, they would have continued with us; but they went out that they might be made manifest, that none of them were of us. 20 But you have an anointing from the Holy One, and you know all things. 21 I have not written to you because you do not know the truth, but because you know it, and that no lie is of the truth. 22 Who is a liar but he who denies that Jesus is the Christ? He is antichrist who denies the Father and the Son. 23 Whoever denies the Son does not have the Father either; he who acknowledges the Son has the Father also. 24 Therefore let that abide in you which you heard from the beginning. If what you heard from the beginning abides in you, you also will abide in the Son and in the Father. 25 And this is the promise that He has promised us—eternal life. 26 These things I have written to you concerning those who try to deceive you. 27 But the anointing which you have received from Him abides in you, and you do not need that anyone teach you; but as the same anointing teaches you concerning all things, and is true, and is not a lie, and just as it has taught you, you will abide in Him. 28 And now, little children, abide in Him, that*

when He appears, we may have confidence and not be ashamed before Him at His coming (1 Jn. 2:18-28).

Here John is warning his readers about apostate teachers and reminding them that the Holy Spirit is sufficient to guard them against heretical teachings. The Church Age is the last hour. Already there are false teachers who promote some of the same doctrine as the coming Antichrist. In John's day, the Gnostics were apostates. They had posed as believers but eventually turned their backs on Christ and the Christian fellowship. By their falling away, they showed that they had never been truly born again.

Believers have an anointing, that is, the teaching ministry of the Holy Spirit. With the Word of God and the Spirit of God, they have all that is necessary for sound doctrine and a godly life. Truth is what God says. Believers have the truth, and know that contrary teachings are a lie.

The acid test is what a person believes about Jesus Christ. To deny that Jesus is the Christ is the spirit of antichrist. If a man doesn't have the Son, he doesn't have the Father either.

So the believers are urged to continue in the sound doctrine which John and the other apostles had taught them, and thus go on in happy fellowship with the Son and the Father. They should remember Christ's unbreakable promise of eternal life to those who have been born again. No conditions are attached.

There is always the danger of deceitful teachers. But the Holy Spirit remains in the children of God, and therefore they do not need the additional "truth" of these Gnostic apostates. The Holy Spirit is their guarantee that believers will abide in Christ.

John appeals to the saints to abide in Christ so that when He appears at the Rapture and the Judgment Seat (His tribunal), John and the other apostles may have confidence and not be ashamed before Him. (John is sure that his readers will be there!) Here it is not a question of confidence versus condemnation but confidence versus shame.

Let us now consider another passage dealing with apostasy.

If anyone sees his brother sinning a sin which does not lead to death, he will ask, and He will give him life for those who commit sin not leading to death. There is sin leading to death. I do not say that he should pray about that (1 Jn. 5:16).

It is almost inevitable that this verse would be used by those who defend the doctrine of conditional security. It seems to leave the door open for the possibility of a Christian committing an unpardonable sin[1] for whom prayer is futile. But is that what it actually says?[2]

First of all, it does not say that it is a believer who commits sin leading to death. The one who commits a sin that does *not* lead to death is a brother, that is, a true child of God. But there is no mention of "brother" in the second part of the verse.

Second, John does not say whether death in this verse is physical or eternal spiritual death. We have to appeal to the context in order to arrive at a proper understanding.

Much of the letter is written to protect the Church from false teachers known as Gnostics. Professing superior knowledge, these men infiltrated Christian assemblies by posing as believers and perhaps even by being baptized. But eventually they abandoned the Christian fellowship altogether, proving that they never had been saved. They manifested themselves as apostates. They sinned unto death. It was impossible to renew them again to repentance (Heb. 6:4-6).

And so John points out here that there are some people for whom there is no use praying. With most sins, it is possible that God will bring the sinner to repentance, and we should pray for this. But apostasy is a sin leading unavoidably to spiritual death, and when someone falls to this point, we need not waste time on our knees for him or her any more.

5 But I want to remind you, though you once knew this, that the Lord, having saved the people out of the land of Egypt, afterward destroyed those who did not believe. 6 And the angels who did not keep their proper domain, but left their own abode, He has reserved in everlasting chains under darkness for the judgment of the great day; 7 as Sodom and Gomorrah, and the cities around them in a similar manner to these, having given themselves over to sexual immorality and gone after strange flesh, are set forth as an example, suffering the vengeance of eternal fire. 8 Likewise also these dreamers defile the flesh, reject authority, and speak evil of dignitaries. 9 Yet Michael the archangel, in contending with the devil, when he disputed about the body of Moses, dared not bring against him a reviling accusation, but said, "The Lord rebuke you!" 10 But these speak evil of whatever they do not know; and whatever they know naturally, like brute beasts, in these things they corrupt themselves. 11 Woe to them! For they have gone in the way of Cain, have run greedily in the error of Balaam for profit, and perished in the rebellion of Korah. 12 These are spots in your love feasts, while they feast with you without fear, serving only themselves. They are clouds without water, carried about by the winds; late autumn trees without fruit, twice dead, pulled up by the roots (Jude 1:5-12).

In his letter, Jude deals almost exclusively with apostates. As we have explained elsewhere, an apostate is one who professes faith in the Lord, then turns against Him with malice and bitterness. He's not a backslider but a *traitor*.

Jude gives these Old Testament examples of apostasy: unbelieving Israelites, angels that sinned, and the people of Sodom and Gomorrah (vv. 5-7). Then he switches to contemporary apostates and their moral uncleanness, defiance of authority, and accusation of officials, which even Michael would not do (vv. 8-9). In showing contempt for governmental powers, they were actually doing it to God.

They are like:

• Cain—rejecting salvation by a substitutionary Sacrifice.

• Balaam—buying and selling religious privileges and benefits.

• The sons of Korah—rebelling against authority and usurping a religious position.

They invaded Christian assemblies like dirty spots, deceitful clouds, and twice dead, fruitless trees.

Such a harsh description does not fit those who ever had genuine faith. These are religious leaders whose lives proved that they never were born again.

ENDNOTES

1 There are three unpardonable sins:
   a. Attributing to the Devil the miracles that Jesus performed by the power of the Holy Spirit, thus blaspheming the Holy Spirit by calling Him the Devil (Mt. 12:24, 31-32).
   b. Professing to embrace the Christian faith, then abandoning it and denying Christ as fully God and fully Man (Heb. 6:4-6, 10:29).
   c. Dying without faith in the Lord Jesus Christ (Jn. 3:18b).

2 This verse has been the despair of commentators because they feel the need for more information. Here are some of the suggested explanations of the one who sins unto death.
   a. A believer who loses his salvation by some unnamed sin.
   b. A believer who suffers physical death because of unconfessed sin. It may be an incurable disease, for instance, that is the result of sexual sin. Prayer is futile.
   c. A believer who commits murder and therefore must suffer the death penalty because God has decreed it (Gen. 9:6).
   d. A believer who commits some egregious public sin that unfits him for further service on earth (Acts 5:1-11) even though he is fit for heaven through the merits of Christ.
   e. An apostate. This is the position we feel best fits the context.

77

14
Profession or Possession?
Part 1

The Bible is a very realistic book. It describes human behavior as it is. It doesn't look through rose-tinted glasses and conclude that everyone is on God's side. Rather it carefully distinguishes between those who are only nominal followers of Christ and those who are genuine believers. It makes a clear distinction between professors and possessors.

When Jesus was on earth, He found these two classes. There were some who believed on Him when they saw the miracles He performed (Jn. 2:23). But He didn't "believe" in them. He is not pleased with the kind of faith that requires signs before a person will believe. He wants the kind of faith that simply believes because He has spoken. Although it says that these people believed on Him, it was not saving faith. They believed in their heads but not in their hearts. They were nothing more than professors.

In His wonderful Bread of Life Discourse, Jesus said, "He who eats My flesh and drinks My blood has eternal life" (Jn. 6:54). To eat His flesh and drink His blood simply means to believe in Him (see v. 47). But some of His disciples were offended by what they called "a hard saying" and they forsook Him (v. 66). By this act of final desertion, they showed that they were disciples in name only. When Jesus asked the Twelve if they also wanted to go away, Peter spoke for all but Judas when he said, "Lord, to whom shall we go? You have the words of eternal life. Also we have come to believe and know that You are the Christ, the Son of the living God" (vv. 68-69). This confession marked them as true disciples of the Lord Jesus.

During the Savior's earthly ministry, there were men who prophesied in His Name, cast out demons in His name, and did many miracles in His name (Mt. 7:22). Yet His verdict on them was, "I *never* knew you." They professed to know Him, but He didn't know them. He exposed them as men who practiced lawlessness (v. 23).

There were others who ate and drank in His presence, and heard Him teach in their streets (Lk. 13:26). They thought that it was enough to associate with the Savior. But once again He said He didn't know them and condemned them as workers of iniquity (v. 27). Outwardly they followed Jesus, but there is no mention of true faith. They just went along for the ride.

In the early days of the Church, there was a classic case of one who was nothing more than a professed follower of Christ. When Philip preached the gospel in Samaria, an influential spiritist named Simon believed and was baptized (Acts 8:13). At first this sounds promising. But remember that there is a pseudo-belief which is not the same as saving faith. We have already seen that kind of faith in John 2:23-25 and 6:66. Even the demons believe (James 2:19). What follows shows that Simon did not have the marks of a true child of God.

When Simon saw that believing Samaritans received the Holy Spirit when the apostles' hands were laid on them, he wanted to buy that power, most likely as a means of gaining a more lucrative trade. Sad to say, he wasn't the last fraud or charlatan who tried to make a lot of money by pretending to be godly (1 Tim. 6:5b)!

Notice how Peter denounced him, and ask yourself if the apostle would say that to a true believer.

Your money perish with you. Peter said, "May you and your money go to hell, for thinking that you can buy God's gift with money" (TEV). Since no true Christian will ever perish (Jn. 3:16), Simon could not have been born again.

You thought that the gift of God could be purchased with money. The gift of God here is the Holy Spirit. Simon wanted to buy the ability to impart the Spirit to others. There is no indication that he himself ever received the Holy Spirit.

80

You have neither part nor portion in this matter. Instead of being a member of the Christian fellowship, he was an outsider, looking in—all because he had no part in the matter of salvation.

Your heart is not right in the sight of God. While this could be said of a backslider, the context suggests a person who needed to be born from above and receive a new heart.

Repent therefore of this wickedness. The word that is used for repent here means turning to God from sin.

Pray God if perhaps the thought of your heart may be forgiven you. God is the One who grants eternal forgiveness to the repentant and believing sinner. But it is as Father that He gives parental forgiveness to one of His children when he confesses. Here it is God, not the Father, who is in view. The word *perhaps* does not suggest uncertainty or unwillingness on God's part but possible stubbornness on Simon's.

You are poisoned by bitterness and bound by iniquity. If a tree is known by its fruit, and if Simon's fruit was extreme wickedness, it raises serious questions concerning his spiritual status.

In response to Peter's stinging indictment, the sorcerer asked the apostle to pray for him. It would have been better if he had repented of his sins and received Christ as Lord and Savior. It seems clear that he was only a professor; he did not have the root of the matter in him.

Here I am reminded of the words of my colleague, Jean Gibson. He has often said, "While we believe in the eternal security of the believer, we don't believe in the eternal security of the profession." Those whose faith is only an acceptance of historical facts should not think that they are in Christ forever. To be a church member is not the same as being a Christian. There is no safety in a head belief—it must be the commitment of a person to a Person.

Several of the parables of our Lord distinguish between profession and possession, between nominal believers and *bona fide* saints. But before studying them individually, we should make a few explanatory remarks concerning the parables of the kingdom of heaven. There are two aspects of the kingdom. First, there is the sphere of outward profession. In this sense, anyone who believes in God or who professes allegiance to Him as King is in the kingdom. But there is also the sphere of inward reality. In order to be a true citizen of the kingdom, a person must be born again (Jn. 3:3, 5). So it's possible to be a subject of the kingdom by profession only, or it's possible to have genuine allegiance to the King.

It is puzzling to think that there is evil and hypocrisy in the Kingdom of heaven until you see that the kingdom in its broadest sense includes profession as well as reality. It is similar to the distinction between Christendom and Christianity. There are a lot of people in Christendom who are not Christians.

Now let's see how the parables distinguish between nominal disciples and true believers.

PARABLE OF THE FOUR SOILS (MT. 13:3-23; LK. 8:4-15)

This parable covers the time from our Lord's ministry on earth to the close of the tribulation period. Jesus is the Sower and the Word of God is the seed. The field is the world. The Word falls on four kinds of soil, that is, it meets four kinds of human responses. The disciples are thus prepared for the fact that not every hearer will become a believer.

The wayside hearer didn't understand the Good News because he didn't want to (see Jn. 7:17) and lost the opportunity to understand it. At first the stony ground hearer received the Word with joy. It would have been better if he had received it with contrition and repentance. When pressured to turn his back on the Word in times of persecution, he did. The thorny ground hearer also showed an initial interest, but he gave a higher priority to worldly interests, pleasures, and deceitful riches. The good ground hearer received the Word, believed it, and bore fruit for God in his own character and in service to others.

The first three soils are unproductive, and thus speak of professors. Only the good ground yields a harvest. It pictures genuine believers, i.e., possessors.

PARABLE OF THE WHEAT AND THE TARES (MT. 13:24-30, 36-43)

This parable also clearly shows the presence of nominal disciples in the kingdom. The devil is a master imitator. He sows tares in the grain field. Just as tares look like wheat, so professors sometimes give every outward appearance of being genuine. But tares are undesirable weeds. There will be tares in the kingdom until Christ comes to reign. Then they will be gathered and judged, and the saints at that time will enter the Millennium.

PARABLE OF THE MUSTARD SEED (MT. 13:31-32)

For a mustard bush to become a tree is abnormal growth. Here it pictures the abnormal growth of Christendom, the sphere where Christian teaching is dominant. The birds of the air, that is, false teachers, rest in its branches. In other words, cultists and heretics, professing to be Christian, invade Christendom.

PARABLE OF THE LEAVEN (MT. 13:33)

Leaven is always a type of evil in the Bible—either evil doctrine (Mk. 8:15, Gal. 5:9) or wicked behavior (1 Cor. 5:6-8). In this parable, a woman mixes leaven in meal. The woman (who should not be teaching doctrine (1 Tim. 2:12) mixes error in the food of God's people. Most cults have some truth but have contaminated it with heresy.

PARABLE OF THE DRAGNET[1] (MT. 13:47-52)

At the end of the Tribulation, the angels will separate the wicked from the just. This will include the separation of nominal believers from those who have been born again. The former will be destroyed. The latter will enter the golden era of peace and prosperity.

PARABLE OF THE UNFORGIVING SERVANT (MT. 18:23-35)

Here is a man who owed an enormous debt to the king. Because he was bankrupt, the king ordered him and his family to be sold into slavery. When he earnestly requested the chance to repay, the king had compassion and freely forgave him the entire debt.

Then the tables turned. The forgiven debtor discovered that one of his co-workers owed him a mere pittance. In spite of the pleas and promises of his debtor, he would not forgive. His master was furious, and ordered him to be turned over to the torturers.

It is clear that the parable is intended for believers since it was in response to Peter's inquiry concerning forgiveness. Since it is for believers, it follows that it is dealing with *parental forgiveness,* not judicial forgiveness. This distinction is important. Judicial or eternal forgiveness is what God the Judge gives to a sinner who believes on the Lord Jesus Christ. It means that Christ, as Substitute, paid the penalty of his sins and he will never have to pay it. Parental or paternal forgiveness is what God, the Father, gives to a sinning believer when he confesses and forsakes his sin. Willingness to forgive is not the gospel for the unsaved. We are not saved by forgiving others. But it *is* vital for believers if they are to walk in fellowship with God, the Father. (Note the words "your heavenly Father" in verse 35.)

So we have seen that the passage is for believers, and that it deals with paternal, not eternal forgiveness. But that being so, how are we to understand verse 34?

And his master was angry, and delivered him to the torturers until he should pay all that was due him.

Does this teach that a believer can lose his salvation?

Notice first what is does not say. He was not delivered to outer darkness, to eternal judgment, or to a doom of fire. He was delivered to unnamed torturers. Who or what are they?

Since the servant was out of fellowship with the Lord, his torturers are the misery and wretchedness that go with that condition. A backslidden Christian is tortured by the quick agony of a guilty conscience, by the shame of dishonoring his Savior, by his loss of the joy of salvation. He is troubled by a blocked prayer life, by sealed lips as far as testimony is concerned, and by the chastening hand of the Lord.

In the parable, the wicked servant was to endure this distress until he had repaid the master 10,000 talents (several million dollars). This would have been clearly impossible. For the child of God there is a better way, that is, to confess and forsake his sin. Then he will receive forgiveness and be restored to fellowship.

PARABLE OF THE WEDDING FEAST (MT. 22:1-14)

It is appropriate that the kingdom of heaven should be compared to a wedding banquet with its joyous celebration. The king's first invitation was rebuffed, so he opened the doors to any who would like to attend. When the king noticed a man who was not wearing proper wedding apparel, he ordered him to be cast out.

To understand this parable we must understand that in those days, suitable clothing for a wedding was provided by the host. So there was no excuse for this guest. When challenged, he was speechless. He represents a person who wants to enjoy the benefits of the kingdom. But he comes in his own righteousness and not in the righteousness which God provides through faith in Christ. He is a Christian in name only.

THE FAITHFUL SERVANT & THE EVIL SERVANT (MT. 24:45-51)

Although this is not called a parable, it has all the marks of one. When the Savior returns to set up His kingdom, He will richly reward those who have cared for His interests, especially in ministering to His household. These are obviously true servants. He calls them faithful, wise, and blessed.

But there will also be other servants who take advantage of His delay by mistreating his fellow servants and carousing with drunkards. They are not *bona fide* servants of Christ, but evil servants who show by their behavior that they have never been born again. They are hypocrites who will share the condemnation of all other pretenders.

PARABLE OF THE TEN VIRGINS (MT. 25:1-13)

The setting of the well-known story of the ten virgins (or bridesmaids) is the close of the Tribulation and the Second Coming of the Lord. There will be two classes of people at that time. The wise virgins represent true believers; the foolish are the unconverted. The crucial difference between them is that the wise ones have oil in their lamps. Oil, of course, is a symbol of the Holy Spirit. If a person does not have the Holy Spirit, he doesn't belong to Christ.

When the bridegroom comes at midnight, the wise virgins are ready and go with him to the marriage banquet,[2] perhaps a figurative expression for the Millennium. The foolish ones plead in vain for admission; but the Lord exposes them as professors, not possessors, saying, "I never knew you." They had *never* been saved through faith in the Lord; He didn't say, "I no longer know you."

PARABLE OF THE TALENTS (MT. 25:14-30)

A talent in the New Testament was a unit of money. In our language, it has acquired the meaning of a gift or ability. In this parable, three men received talents from a wealthy man according to their abilities to invest for him. When he returned from an extended trip, he asked for an accounting. The first two had doubled the amount entrusted to them, so he gave them responsibility over many projects. The third steward had buried his one talent, excusing himself by saying, "I knew you to be a hard man, reaping where you have not sown, and gathering where you have not scattered seed." If that's the way he felt about his boss, he should have deposited the money with bankers so that there would be some return on the money. As punishment he would be cast into outer darkness where there is weeping and gnashing of teeth.

The first two men represent true servants of the Lord who faithfully invest for the kingdom. The third is a servant in name only. This is seen in the way he spoke about his lord. "You are a hard person, unfairly expecting too much, and profiting at the expense of others." No true believer could ever accuse our Lord of that.

It is seen in the Lord's description of him. He was wicked, lazy, and unprofitable. His sins were false accusation and neglect (Heb. 2:3). It is seen in his doom. He was cast into outer darkness. In

86

short, he was a professing servant but not a true one.

In addition to the above examples of profession and possession, there are other passages which speak of people who claim to be Christians but show by their lives that they are not.

DEPARTING FROM THE FAITH (1 TIM. 4:1)

In 1 Timothy 4:1, the apostle Paul foresees that in the latter times some will depart from the faith. Those who believe that a Christian can be lost use this verse as a proof text. They reason that if some depart from the faith, they once kept it but no longer do so. How can they depart from something they never held?

The answer is that they depart from a say-so faith. They could be nominal Christians without ever having experienced the new birth. In today's world, anyone who believes in God and is kind to his mother qualifies as a Christian. We all know that there are members in most evangelical churches who are still in their sins. When a well-known minister was asked if all the people in his congregation were members of God's family, he replied, "I wouldn't want to be handcuffed to some of them when they die." Which was his whimsical way of saying that he wouldn't want to go where they were going.

Now these people could certainly depart from the faith by departing from Christian fellowship, Christian teaching, and Christian morality. Those who depart from the faith in 1 Timothy turn to:

- demonic fellowship—deceiving spirits;
- demonic teaching—doctrines of demons;
- demonic morality—speaking lies in hypocrisy and having a seared conscience.

They depart from the faith to take up with spiritism. There is no suggestion that a believer will do this. Rather, Timothy is warned that this is what it will be like when the great apostasy sweeps across the world, and he is directed to warn the brethren that this will take place.

OVERTHROW THE FAITH (1 TIM. 1:20; 2 TIM. 2:16-18)

What about Hymenaeus and Philetus? Some people use them to show that saved people can subsequently be lost. They make two big assumptions: first, that these two men were genuine believers; and, second, that they lost their salvation. But we cannot win a case by assumptions.

When it says in 1 Timothy 1:19, "having faith and a good conscience, which some having rejected..." the "which" refers to "a good conscience," not to "faith." This is clear in the original language.

Often we have to say about people like Hymenaeus and Philetus what Paul said about the Galatians, "I have doubts about you" (Gal. 4:20). It is interesting and perhaps significant that immediately after describing these two men, the apostle says, "The Lord knows those who are His" (2 Tim. 2:19). We can't always tell for sure, but the Lord knows. And if anyone professes to belong to Christ, he or she should demonstrate it by departing from iniquity.

Here is what we can know definitely about Hymenaeus and Philetus

• They strayed concerning the faith. To stray is not the same as to abandon. Many believers have strayed by following religious novelties and quirky teaching. It's possible to be a Christian and be doctrinally unstable.

• They said the resurrection had already taken place. They didn't deny the resurrection but were wrong about its nature and timing. They probably applied it to the soul whereas the word always refers to the body. They taught that it had happened at who-knows-what time, whereas we know it is still future. It's possible to be a Christian and still be quite ignorant.

• They overthrow the faith of some. This may mean that they left a trail of confusion and subversion. It is possible to be a Christian and yet be a bad worker.

• Hymenaeus had suffered shipwreck concerning the faith (1 Tim. 1:19-20). He may not have been a deserter but he made a failure of his life and service. Paul said he had delivered him to Satan so that he might learn not to blaspheme. The only other time this judicial action of delivery to Satan is mentioned is in 1 Corinthians 5:5. Here it is in reference to a believer who had committed immorality. He was to be excommunicated from the church and thus placed in Satan's territory "that his spirit may be saved in the day of the Lord Jesus." So it is possible that Hymenaeus was a believer. It is possible to be a Christian and be a spiritual shipwreck.

• Alexander is mentioned in 1 Timothy 1:20 along with Hymenaeus. He also rejected a good conscience and made shipwreck concerning the Christian faith. Paul delivered him to Satan so that he also would learn not to blaspheme. We do not know if he was the same Alexander who did Paul much harm (2 Tim. 4:14).

In order to make a definite decision concerning these men, we really need to know more. So we have to place them in a file labeled "Awaiting further information."

DEMAS (2 TIM. 4:10)

Demas was one of Paul's colleagues during his first imprisonment in Rome (Philemon 1:24; see also Col. 4:14). Later he forsook the apostle, "having loved this present world" (2 Tim. 4:10). Is this a case of a true believer losing his salvation? Was Demas a professor or a possessor?

The fact that he served with Paul does not prove that he had ever been converted. Judas served with Christ, and many others who claimed to serve Christ later proved that they did not belong to Him.

The clearest indication that he was not a genuine child of God is that he loved this present world. The apostle John states in his nononsense manner, "If anyone loves the world, the love of the Father is not in him" (1 Jn. 2:15b).

The only mitigating thing is that although Demas left Paul, it doesn't say he left Christ. But this is overweighed by the fact that he loved the world. So there is good reason to believe that Demas did not know the Lord.

Many servants of the Lord have had an experience similar to

Paul's. They know the sorrow of finding that a loved and trusted fellow-worker was a counterfeit after all.

ENDNOTES

1 We have passed over the parable of the hidden treasure and the parable of the pearl of great price since they do not bear on the subject of profession and possession.

2 Most versions have "marriage feast" rather than simply "marriage," as in the KJV and NKJV. The marriage had already taken place in heaven at the Rapture. Now the Bridegroom comes with His bride, the Church, to the banquet.

15
Profession or Possession?
Part 2

Two New Testament epistles give special attention to the difference between a professor and a possessor. One of these is First John. The people to whom John was directly writing were genuine believers. However, they were troubled by a group of false teachers called Gnostics.[1]

These arrogant religionists at first pretended to be Christians. But problems soon developed. They claimed to have a special knowledge from God, and to be more spiritually advanced than the ordinary, simple believers. They denied the deity of Christ, they lived in flagrant immorality, they treated believers with contempt, and they meanwhile claimed to be sinless (the grand slam of apostasy!).[2]

John wrote his letter to reassure the genuine believers that there was a difference between them and these heretics. The believers, who worshiped Christ as the Son of God, who lived lives of righteousness and love, and who confessed their sins, were the true possessors of the Kingdom. The Gnostics, by contrast, were false professors of the faith.

5 This is the message which we have heard from Him and declare to you, that God is light and in Him is no darkness at all. 6 If we say that we have fellowship with Him, and walk in darkness, we lie and do not practice the truth. 7 But if we walk in the light as He is in the light, we have fellowship with one another, and the blood of Jesus Christ His Son cleanses us from all sin. 8 If we say that we have no sin, we deceive ourselves, and the truth is not in us. 9 If we confess our sins, He is faithful and just

to forgive us our sins and to cleanse us from all unrighteousness.
10 If we say that we have not sinned, we make Him a liar, and
His word is not in us. 1 My little children, these things I write to
you, so that you may not sin. And if anyone sins, we have an Ad-
vocate with the Father, Jesus Christ the righteous. 2 And He
Himself is the propitiation for our sins, and not for ours only but
also for the whole world. 3 Now by this we know that we know
Him, if we keep His commandments. 4 He who says, "I know
Him," and does not keep His commandments, is a liar, and the
truth is not in him. 5 But whoever keeps His word, truly the love
of God is perfected in him. By this we know that we are in Him.
6 He who says he abides in Him ought himself also to walk just
as He walked. 7 Brethren, I write no new commandment to you,
but an old commandment which you have had from the begin-
ning. The old commandment is the word which you heard from
the beginning. 8 Again, a new commandment I write to you,
which thing is true in Him and in you, because the darkness is
passing away, and the true light is already shining. 9 He who
says he is in the light, and hates his brother, is in darkness until
now. 10 He who loves his brother abides in the light, and there is
no cause for stumbling in him. 11 But he who hates his brother is
in darkness and walks in darkness, and does not know where he
is going, because the darkness has blinded his eyes (1 Jn. 1:5-
2:11).

In the process of explaining each verse of this passage simply,
we will answer verses that supposedly teach conditional salvation.

1:5 From the outset of His public ministry, Jesus taught that God
is light (morally perfect) and there is no darkness (impurity) in Him.

1:6 Anyone who professes fellowship with Him and lives in sin
is lying, and does not practice the truth of the Christian faith.

1:7 If we live a clean life, as He is holy, then we have fellowship
with the Father, the Son, and fellow believers, and we are continually cleansed from all sin (by confessing and forsaking it).

1:8 If we say we don't have a sin nature or haven't committed sinful acts, we deceive ourselves and we don't tell the truth.

1:9 If we confess our sin, He is faithful to His promise and has a righteous basis to forgive our sin, and to cleanse us from everything that isn't right.

1:10 If we say we have been sinless, we call God a liar and deny the truth of the Word.

2:1 God's perfect standard is that we should not sin at all. (He couldn't say anything less than this.) But He has made provision in case we do sin. (He is still our Father even if we sin.) We have an honest Lawyer to plead our cause.

2:2 And by His sacrifice our Defense Attorney has fully satisfied God's claims against our sins. His death is sufficient for the sins of the whole world, but those sins are forgiven only when a sinner receives the Lord Jesus as God and Savior.

2:3 One of the marks of a true believer is that he habitually obeys the Lord.

2:4 Anyone who says he is a Christian but habitually disobeys the Lord's commandments is a false professor.

2:5 God's love has achieved its goal in the one who makes it a habit to obey Him. That is a proof that the person is saved.

2:6 Talk should be matched by walk. A person's life should be in harmony with his profession. Anyone who says he is in Christ should live a Christian life.

2:7 The command to love one another dates back to the beginning of Christ's earthly ministry. John's readers had heard it from the outset.

2:8 But there is a sense in which it is new or fresh. Whereas it was always true in the life of our Lord, now it is true in believers as well because the light of Christianity is shining in the saints.

2:9 But the darkness is still in anyone who hates his brother. He always was in darkness and still is.

2:10 The one who loves his brother is living in the light. He doesn't stumble and he doesn't cause others to stumble.

2:11 Anyone who hates his brother is blind. He walks in the darkness, and doesn't know where he is going.

In most of these verses, John is distinguishing between a real believer and a mere professor (note the repetition of "he who *says*" (2:4, 6, 9).

Do not love the world or the things in the world. If anyone loves the world, the love of the Father is not in him. For all that is in the world—the lust of the flesh, the lust of the eyes, and the pride of life—is not of the Father but is of the world. And the world is passing away, and the lust of it; but he who does the will of God abides forever (1 Jn. 2:15-17).

One of the marks of a true Christian is that he does not love the world in the sense that he is not controlled by that love. Actually most believers have been attracted by the world to some degree. But if anyone lives to indulge the lust of the flesh, the lust of the eyes, and the pride of life, he cannot at the same time be a lover of the Father. He is living for a doomed system. Only those who live to do the will of God will abide forever.

There is nothing here to support conditional salvation. The contrast is between world-lovers and God-lovers, between the saved and the lost.

But why warn Christians about loving the world if they can't do it? Because the world can have a negative influence on God's people even if it cannot have first place in their lives.

If you know that He is righteous, you know that everyone who practices righteousness is born of Him. Behold what manner of love the Father has bestowed on us, that we should be called children of God! Therefore the world does not know us, because it did not know Him. Beloved, now we are children of God; and it has not yet been revealed what we shall be, but we know that when He is revealed, we shall be like Him, for we shall see Him as He is. And everyone who has this hope in Him purifies himself, just as He is pure. Whoever commits sin also commits lawlessness, and sin is lawlessness. And you know that He was manifested to take away our sins, and in Him there is no sin. Whoever abides in Him does not sin. Whoever sins has neither seen

94

> *Him nor known Him. Little children, let no one deceive you. He who practices righteousness is righteous, just as He is righteous. He who sins is of the devil, for the devil has sinned from the beginning. For this purpose the Son of God was manifested, that He might destroy the works of the devil. Whoever has been born of God does not sin, for His seed remains in him; and he cannot sin, because he has been born of God* (1 Jn. 2:29-3:9).

Like Father, like son. It is a fact of natural life that like begets like. Children are born in the image and after the likeness of their parents. So it is in the spiritual realm. Since the Father is righteous, His children will practice righteousness.

The thought of "those who are born of Him" (2:29) launches John into an expression of wonder that we should ever be the children of God. No wonder the world doesn't recognize or appreciate who we are. It didn't recognize our Lord.

Then in a wonderful outburst on eternal security, the apostle expresses the unconditional fact that we (his readers and all true believers) will be changed into the likeness of Christ by gazing at Him. No question about it! In the meantime the prospect serves as a purifying hope. And we must remember that this hope is certain because it is based of God's Word.

This brings John to another mark of a believer. Although he still sins, he does not live under the dominion of sin. His lifestyle is not characteristically sinful. He is not a habitual sinner. The following paraphrase seeks to express this.

4. Whoever practices sin also practices lawlessness, and sin is lawlessness.[3]

5. And you know that He was manifested to take away our sins, and in Him there is no sin.

6. Whoever abides in Him, that is, a Christian, does not go on sinning habitually. Whoever is dominated by sin has neither seen Him nor known Him.

7. Little children, he who practices righteousness is righteous, just as He is righteous.

8. He whose life is sinful is of the devil because he has gone on sinning from the beginning. This is why the Son of God appeared on earth, that He might destroy the works of the devil.[4]

9. Whoever has been born of God does not live in sin, because his seed, that is, the life of Christ, remains in him, and he cannot go on sinning, because he is a child of God.[5]

1 John 3:4-9, 5:18 are handled in greater detail in the chapter titled "Occasional or Habitual?"

Now we turn to James' letter as he deals with profession and reality. It is written in a tone markedly different from that of First John. James was addressing people whose lives did not seem to back up their professions. And so he wrote rather bluntly—which was necessary to break through the hardened hearts of many of his readers. He warned them that good works were needed to demonstrate their claim to be believers.

James 2:14-26 has historically been one of the more controversial passages in all of Scripture. Some claim that it teaches that we are saved by works, or at least partly by works. Conditional salvationists use it to say that our salvation is *preserved* by works. Let's see how our understanding of the difference between professors and possessors helps us to clarify it.

What does it profit, my brethren, if someone says he has faith but does not have works? Can faith save him? If a brother or sister is naked and destitute of daily food, and one of you says to them, "Depart in peace, be warmed and filled," but you do not give them the things which are needed for the body, what does it profit? Thus also faith by itself, if it does not have works, is dead. But someone will say, "You have faith, and I have works." Show me your faith without your works, and I will show you my faith by my works. You believe that there is one God. You do well. Even the demons believe—and tremble! But do you want to know, O foolish man, that faith without works is dead? Was not Abraham our father justified by works when he offered Isaac his son on the altar? Do you see that faith was working together with his

works, and by works his faith was made perfect? And the Scrip-
ture was fulfilled which says, "Abraham believed God, and it
was accounted to him for righteousness." And he was called the
friend of God. You see then that a man is justified by works, and
not by faith only. Likewise, was not Rahab the harlot also justi-
fied by works when she received the messengers and sent them
out another way? For as the body without the spirit is dead, so
faith without works is dead also (James 2:14-26).

James' words are sometimes used to show that faith in Christ is
not enough. One's initial faith must be continually followed by
good works in order to be effective. Thus faith without works is
dead. But let's examine the verses carefully and see what they really
say.

Verse 14. It does not say that this man has faith. He *says* he has
faith. It is a say-so faith but there has never been a change in his
life. Works here are not a condition for his continued salvation.
They are an evidence of saving faith. When Christ comes into a life,
He makes a difference. It is not enough to profess faith. A person
must truly repent of his sins and trust Christ as Lord and Savior.

Verses 15-17 illustrate and emphasize the uselessness of words
without deeds. So is a faith of words only, one that does not result
in the fruit of divine life.

Verse 18. A true believer challenges a man with nominal faith to
demonstrate his faith without corresponding works. It can't be done.
Faith is invisible. It is works that reveal the existence of genuine
faith. So the believer can rightly say, "I will show you my faith by
my works."

Verse 19. A mere intellectual faith, a belief in obvious facts, is
not sufficient. Even the demons believe in the existence of one God
and tremble. But that does not save them.

Verse 20. We are *not* saved by works. We are not saved by faith
plus works. But we are saved by the kind of faith that *results* in a
life of good works. The good works do not contribute to the continuance of salvation. If they did, that would be a form of salvation by

works. Rather they are the inevitable outcome of true, saving faith.

Verses 21-24. James now cites Abraham as an example of genuine faith. In Genesis 15:6, "he believed in the Lord, and He accounted it to him for righteousness." In other words, he was justified by faith. Years later—perhaps 20 years later—he was justified by works when he showed willingness to offer Isaac as a burnt offering to God (Gen. 22:10). His work demonstrated the reality of his faith.

But notice that it was not what we would ordinarily consider a "good work." It was the intention to kill his son. The only reason it was good is because it demonstrated faith in God.

Verse 25. The same is true of Rahab. Her work was treason, usually a bad work. It didn't save her or contribute to her salvation, but it was proof that her faith in the God of Israel was genuine.

Verse 26. James wraps up the subject by reminding us that just as the (visible) body without the (invisible) spirit is dead, so faith (which is invisible) without works (visible) is dead also.

In general this is not a good passage to use in seeking to prove conditional security. It does not prove that good works must be *added* to faith in order to earn continued salvation. But it does emphasize that where there is true faith, there will be works to make it manifest.

ENDNOTES

1 Their name comes from the Greek word for "knowledge" (*gnōsis*). They thought they knew so much more than orthodox believers.

2 Gnosticism later developed many subdivisions. For example, some were licentious and others were actually ascetic.

3 The word "commits" (whoever commits sin) in the NKJV is unfortunate. It is the practice of sin that is in view. It is contrasted with "practices righteousness" in 2:29.

4 In verses 6, 8, and 9, the NKJV could imply that a Christian does not sin at all. This, of course, is contradicted by 1 John 1:8-10; 2:1. It is sin as a lifestyle that is in view. It is contrasted with the practice of righteousness in 3:7, 10. And it is illustrated by the behavior of the devil; he "has sinned from the beginning." It is his characteristic behavior.

5 Another interpretation that accepts eternal security sees this as saying that the new nature ("born of God") cannot sin at all.

16
Law or Grace?

Ultimately the question of the believer's security hinges on one's understanding of the grace of God. Both sides of the controversy would agree that salvation is by grace, but there's a difference in what they *mean* by grace.

It is important to remember that there are only two principles on which salvation could be offered—law and grace.

The principle of law means that there is something meritorious we can and must do in order to earn salvation or to keep it. The principle of grace says that salvation is God's unmerited favor from beginning to end. There is nothing we can and must do to earn, deserve, or keep it. It's a free gift, received by faith, and is completely apart from works.

The two principles are totally opposed. Paul makes it clear that they cannot be mixed, "...if by grace, then it is no longer of works; otherwise grace is no longer grace. But if it is of works, it is no longer grace; otherwise work is no longer work" (Rom. 11:6). Salvation cannot be partly by law-keeping and partly by grace.

Those who believe in conditional security would agree that *initial* salvation is by grace but they also believe that a person can forfeit that salvation either by deciding to stop believing or by serious or continued sin. But their writings betray the fact that they try to mix law and grace. For instance, one of their leading advocates says:

> The Lordship of Jesus over self, life, and possessions must be acknowledged if we are to know Him as Savior.[1]

In another place he writes:

Keeping His commandments is not optional for a man who would enter into life. It is an essential aspect of saving faith.[2]

And again:

There is definitely a sense in which man is 'his own savior.'[3]

In general, the argument is that we must believe and keep on believing. We must endure. We must continue. We must persevere. We must hold fast. The emphasis is on *what we must do,* not on what God *has done.* It is on human effort, not on divine gift. This is works. It is the principle of law. It says that there is something man must do to earn or keep his salvation.

Some of the Galatian Christians had been saved by grace through faith and apart from law-keeping. But they believed false teachers who said they now had to keep the law in order to hold on to their salvation. Paul rebuked them: "Are you so foolish? Having begun in the Spirit, are you now made perfect by the flesh?" (Gal. 3:3).

They should have remembered that salvation is a free gift, received by faith, and it's completely apart from works. Christ finished the work on the cross. We must not try to add to His finished work. The same One who begins this good work performs it until the end (see Phil. 1:6). The preservation of our souls is God's responsibility (1 Tim. 1:12).

Of course, this inevitably raises the question, "What happens when a child of God sins?" One view is that he loses his salvation and must be saved again. The other position is that his fellowship with God is broken and remains broken until he confesses and forsakes his sin. Those who hold the first view believe that God's method of producing holiness is to put believers in fear of losing their salvation. Those who belong to the grace school insist that love for the Lord and not fear of punishment is the strongest motive.

Does this mean that those who are grounded in the doctrine of grace can go on living in sin? God forbid! Rather it raises the question of whether they were ever saved at all.

So here you have the two positions. One says that a Christian who sins repeatedly is lost (the seriousness or extent of the sin is not specified). The other says that if sin is a person's characteristic behavior, if it is the dominating influence in his life, he is not a member of God's family. If he is truly saved, he will be pressured by the Lord to confess his sin and receive the Father's forgiveness.

Here are some verses that are used to suggest that believers earn or forfeit their salvation by their performance:

But he who endures to the end shall be saved (Mt. 24:13).

In context this verse has special application to the Great Tribulation. Some might be tempted to think that they could escape persecution and martyrdom if they denied that they were believers. But the Lord encourages them that true safety lies in enduring to the end.

However, even if applied to the present day believer, it simply shows that true faith always has the quality of permanence. Faith may have temporary relapses, but it will live on. A believer may fall seven times but he will rise again (see Prov. 24:16). Perseverance is characteristic of a true child of God. "Those who trust in the Lord are like Mount Zion, which cannot be removed, but abides forever" (Ps. 125:1).

To suggest that we receive eternal salvation by enduring is in conflict with over 30 verses that teach that we are saved by faith in the Lord.

Then Jesus said to those Jews who believed Him, "If you abide in My word, you are my disciples indeed. And you shall know the truth, and the truth shall make you free" (Jn. 8:31-32).

Jesus spoke these words to some Jewish people who had just believed in Him. They could prove the reality of their faith by abiding in His Word. This would show that they were disciples in the true sense of the word, and they would enjoy the liberating power of the Word.

Most assuredly, I say to you, if anyone keeps My word he shall never see death (Jn. 8:51).

To keep the words of the Lord Jesus is another way of saying to believe on Him. We know this by comparing this verse with John 11:26. In the first, the one who keeps His Word will never die. In the second, the person who believes on Him will never die. *Things equal to the same thing are equal to each other.*

ENDNOTES

1   Robert Shank, *Life in the Son: A Study of the Doctrine of Perseverance.* Springfield, Missouri: Westcott Publishers, 1961, p. 16.

2   Ibid., p. 219.

3   Ibid., p. 96.

17
Fellowship or Relationship?

Sometimes when we come up against problems in the New Testament, the solution lies in distinguishing between relationship and fellowship. When we speak of relationship, we mean the kinship that exists between God the Father and a believer that is established by the new birth. Fellowship refers to the happy family spirit that exists between a Christian and the members of the Godhead when there is no unconfessed sin, when there is agreement, when they walk together in unity. A passage that distinguishes between relationship and fellowship is found in John 13.

1 Now before the feast of the Passover, when Jesus knew that His hour had come that He should depart from this world to the Father, having loved His own who were in the world, He loved them to the end. 2 And supper being ended, the devil having already put it into the heart of Judas Iscariot, Simon's son, to betray Him, 3 Jesus, knowing that the Father had given all things into His hands, and that He had come from God and was going to God, 4 rose from supper and laid aside His garments, took a towel and girded Himself. 5 After that, He poured water into a basin and began to wash the disciples' feet, and to wipe them with the towel with which He was girded. 6 Then He came to Simon Peter. And Peter said to Him, "Lord, are You washing my feet?" 7 Jesus answered and said to him, "What I am doing you do not understand now, but you will know after this." 8 Peter said to Him, "You shall never wash my feet!" Jesus answered him, "If I do not wash you, you have no part with Me." 9 Simon Peter said to Him, "Lord, not my feet only, but also my hands and my head!" 10 Jesus said to him, "He who is bathed needs only to wash his feet, but is completely clean; and you are clean, but not all of you." 11 For He knew who would betray Him; therefore He said, "You are not all clean" (vv. 1-11).

What an amazing incident! Here we see the Mighty Maker of the universe donning the apron of a slave and bending to wash His disciples' feet. When He came to Peter, the impetuous apostle protested that it was inappropriate for the Master to wash the feet of a disciple. "You shall never wash my feet," he said.

The Lord Jesus answered, "If I do not wash you, you have no part with me" (v. 8). That being the case, Peter asked for a complete bath, not a partial washing.

Jesus answered, "He who is bathed needs only to wash his feet, but is completely clean..."

The Savior's words in verse 8 are sometimes used to support the doctrine of conditional security. In order to understand them correctly we must see them in their setting.

There is a difference between the bath and the footwashing. The former is the bath of regeneration, as mentioned in Titus 3:5: "Not by works of righteousness that we have done, but according to His mercy He saved us, through the washing [bath] of regeneration and renewing of the Holy Spirit." In a word, the bath is salvation. It takes place only once.

But then there is the foot-washing. If the bath takes place only once, the footwashing takes place repeatedly. In the Christian life we daily commit sin and contract defilement. We need constant cleansing by the application of the Word of God to our lives. This speaks of the maintenance of fellowship. While relationship is an unbreakable chain, fellowship is a thread that is easily broken. Sin breaks fellowship, and we need the ministry of the Word to cleanse our walk.

In Paul's day, people would go to the public baths for a thorough cleaning. But even in walking home in their sandals, their feet would get soiled again. This illustrates the bath and the footwashing. The bath is salvation; the footwashing is sanctification.

Since the bath of regeneration takes place only once, Peter didn't need it again. He was already saved. This refutes the idea of a person being saved, losing his salvation through sin, then being saved again.

In the act of regeneration, a relationship is established. God is the Father and the believer is His child. This relationship is indissoluble. Just as in the natural relationship, it is forever. Sin does not break the relationship. If a believer sins, God is still his Father (1 Jn. 2:1b).

When the Lord said to Peter, "If I do not wash you, you have no part with Me," he was speaking about fellowship, not relationship. Apart from the constant cleansing by the Word, Peter could not walk in fellowship with his Master.

Cleansing by the Word does not contradict cleansing by the blood of Jesus Christ, God's Son. As we appropriate the Word, it leads us to confess and forsake sin, "and the blood of Jesus Christ, His Son cleanses us from all sin" (1 Jn. 1:7c). So the two are not contradictory but complementary.

107

18
Salvation or Discipleship?

Failure to distinguish between verses that deal with salvation and those that are concerned with discipleship has caused confusion in the area of the believer's security.

When God promises eternal life to sinners on the basis of faith, you can know that the soul's salvation is in view. But when the Lord is speaking to true disciples, and urges them to lives of dedication, good works, and sacrifice, He is dealing with discipleship.

There are no degrees of salvation. A person is either saved or he isn't. No believer is more fit for heaven than another. If anyone has Jesus Christ as his Lord and Savior, he is as fit for heaven as God can make him. He is not saved by his own merits but by the merits of the Savior. It is "in Christ" that he is accepted, complete, and made fit for heaven.

We have already quoted verses that clearly deal with salvation. To mention just a few: Matthew 11:28; Jn. 1:12; 3:16; 3:36; 5:24; 6:47; Acts 16:31; Romans 10:9.

But while there are no degrees of fitness for heaven, there are degrees of discipleship. For instance, there are babes, young men, and fathers (1 Jn. 2:12-14). Some are still feeding on milk while others eat solid food (Heb. 5:12-14). A disciple is a learner, and obviously there are some Christians who learn more than others.

When a person is first saved, he starts out in God's school of discipleship. The more he studies and obeys the Word, the faster he advances from one grade to another. The ideal of discipleship is to become more like the Master.

Jesus spoke of those who abide in His Word and thus become disciples indeed. The expression "disciples indeed" may indicate the ideal. No one is a perfect disciple, but anyone can become a disciple indeed by obeying the hard sayings of the Lord as well as His simple commands.

Listen to some of the hard sayings:

If anyone desires to come after Me, let him deny himself, and take up his cross daily, and follow Me (Lk. 9:23).

If anyone comes to Me and does not hate his father and mother, wife and children, brothers and sisters, yes, and his own life also, he cannot be My disciple (Lk. 14:26).

This means that an ideal disciple, one in the fuller sense of the word, puts Christ before human relationships.

So likewise, whoever of you does not forsake all that he has cannot be My disciple (Lk. 14:33).

Now it should be clear that these verses are not the gospel. They are not good news for lost sinners. It requires divine life to obey them, and the only way to get that divine life is to be born again. Without it, these verses can only condemn.

But they are good instruction for believers who want to walk in close fellowship with the Lord Jesus Christ. They present ideals toward which all Christians should strive.

Here are some other verses that deal with discipleship and not with salvation:

And his master was angry, and delivered him to the torturers until he should pay all that was due to him. So My heavenly Father also will do to you if each of you, from his heart, does not forgive his brother his trespasses (Mt. 18:34-35).

As explained elsewhere, it does not say that the disciple who would not forgive would be delivered to Satan or to hell, but rather to the torturers, that is, to all the miseries of being out of fellowship with God. Notice that the punishment is only temporary, not eternal—"until he had paid all." He would be restored to fellowship as soon as he confessed and forsook his sin and made restitution.

And everyone who has left houses or brothers or sisters or father or mother or children or lands, for My name's sake, shall receive a hundredfold, and inherit eternal life (Mt. 19:29).

This means a greater capacity for enjoying eternal life and greater rewards. The life itself is received by faith in Christ.

He who loves his life will lose it, and he who hates his life in this world will keep it for eternal life (Jn. 12:25).

Once again it is not the possession of eternal life that is at stake but greater rewards and a fuller enjoyment of it in heaven.

So we can summarize in this way. Whenever you find verses that invite sinners to put their faith in Christ, you know that the subject is salvation. When you find exhortations to love, holiness, sacrificial living, perseverance, or other Christian virtues, you know that discipleship is in view.

19
Fruitbearing or Salvation?

1 I am the true vine, and My Father is the vinedresser. 2 Every branch in Me that does not bear fruit He takes away; and every branch that bears fruit He prunes, that it may bear more fruit. 3 You are already clean because of the word which I have spoken to you. 4 Abide in Me, and I in you. As the branch cannot bear fruit of itself, unless it abides in the vine, neither can you, unless you abide in Me. 5 I am the vine, you are the branches. He who abides in Me, and I in him, bears much fruit; for without Me you can do nothing. 6 If anyone does not abide in Me, he is cast out as a branch and is withered; and they gather them and throw them into the fire, and they are burned (Jn. 15:1-6).

The subject here is *fruitbearing,* not salvation! It's not a gospel message for sinners but an exhortation to saints for close personal fellowship with the Lord. Salvation is a free gift, but a life of spiritual intimacy with the Lord Jesus is for those who abide in His love and obey His commandments.

In contrast to Israel, the Lord Jesus is the true vine. That nation brought forth only wild grapes (Isa. 5:2, 4). God the Father is the Vinedresser. All believers are branches on the vine. They draw their life, sustenance, and productivity from Him.

The great question in verse 2 is the meaning of the phrase "takes away." To the Arminian it is proof that a true believer can be consigned to hell. Some think that the fruitless branch is a false professor. Others say it means to remove from service through sickness or death (Acts 5:1-10; 1 Cor. 11:30). The interpretations are legion. May I add another one to the number.

The word translated "takes away" could just as accurately be rendered "lifts up" or "props up."[1] In fact, it would be much more in keeping with the science of viticulture. The picture is of a branch that is on the ground, muddied and infested with insects. The vine-dresser lifts it up and perhaps attaches it to a stake so that it can get on with the business of fruit-bearing.

The Greek word means "to lift up" in the following passages where it could not possibly mean "to take away":

Luke 17:13: "they *lifted* up their voices."
John 11:41: "Jesus *lifted* up His eyes."
Acts 4:24: "they *raised* their voices to God."
Revelation 10:5: "the angel... *lifted* up his hand to heaven."

Here are other verses where the word means "to lift up" rather than "to take away":

Matthew 9:6: "...then He said to the paralytic, 'Arise, *take* up your bed, and go to your house....'" (See also Mk. 2:3, 9, 11, 12; Lk. 5:24-25; Jn. 5:8-12.)

Matthew 11:29: "*Take* My yoke upon you and learn from Me...."

Matthew 14:20: "...and they *took* up twelve baskets of the fragments that remained." (See also Matthew 15:37; Mk. 6:43; 8:8, 19-20).

Matthew 16:24: "...If anyone desires to come after Me, let him deny himself, and *take* up his cross, and follow Me." (Also Matthew 27:32; Mk. 8:34; 10:21; 15:21.)

Matthew 17:27: "...go to the sea, cast in a hook, and *take* the fish that comes up first...."

Mark 16:18: "they will *take* up serpents...."

John 8:59: "Then they *took* up stones to throw at Him...."

Even in verses where the word is translated "take away," the additional meaning is evident from the context. (See Matthew 14:12; 22:13; 24:39; Mk. 6:29; Lk. 8:12; Jn. 11:39; 19:38.) Only rarely does it mean to take away to destruction.

114

The latter part of verse 2 tells how the Heavenly Vinedresser prunes vines that bear fruit. This insures that all needed nutrients will go to the fruit and not be dissipated in leaves and branches. Pruning here is equivalent to child-training in Hebrews 12. It means getting rid of everything that diminishes spiritual growth and encouraging fruit for God in every possible way.

The disciples were already clean morally and spiritually because the Master had taught them the Word of God.

In the words, "Abide in Me, and I in you," the first part is an exhortation, the second half a statement of fact. Every indicative inevitably leads to an imperative. A believer can no more produce the fruit of a Christlike life than a branch can grow grapes apart from the vine. Abiding is equivalent to obeying (Jn. 15:10, 1 Jn. 3:24). It also speaks of dependence. The branch is dependent on the vine for its life and nourishment. As a believer (branch) lives in abiding fellowship with the indwelling Christ (Vine), he bears much fruit. Notice the progression:

> Much fruit
> More fruit
> Fruit
> No fruit

Apart from the living Vine, a human branch can do *nothing*. This is true not only in the matter of fruitbearing, but as far as salvation is concerned as well.

Verse 6 is a darling of those who read it to say: "If anyone does not abide in Me, he is cast out by God and is withered, and God gathers them and throws them in the fires of hell, and they are burnt." But that is not what the Lord Jesus said.

- He did not say the believer is cast out by God and withered.
- He did not say that God gathers them.
- He did not say that He casts them into hell.

The branch that does not abide in the vine is a believer who does not walk in obedience to the Lord and, as a result, loses his testimo-

115

ny. He is rejected as a branch and is withered, not by God but by men. Unbelievers scorn his profession of being a Christian. They gather his name, reputation, and Christian profession and throw them into the fire. Notice again that it does not say that *God* casts them into the fire. It is the people of the world who have nothing but contempt for one with high talk and low walk. The believer's testimony is burned, and he himself is like salt that has lost its savor (Mt. 5:13) or like a church which is no longer a light bearer (Rev. 2:5).

David is an illustration. He was a true believer, but he did not abide in the Vine. As a result, he fell into deep sin, and gave occasion for the enemies of the Lord to blaspheme (see 2 Sam. 12:14). He didn't lose his salvation but he did lose his good reputation and suffered the Lord's chastening.

ENDNOTE

1 The Logos 21 version of John's Gospel, *Living Water,* translates the verb "props up."

20
Continuation or Preservation?

Many passages seem to support conditional security if we fail to recognize that when the apostles encouraged the new believers to continue strongly in the Christian life they were not necessarily warning them that they might fall away from it completely. Two straightforward examples of this are found in the book of Acts:

And the hand of the Lord was with them, and a great number believed and turned to the Lord. Then news of these things came to the ears of the church in Jerusalem, and they sent out Barnabas to go as far as Antioch. When he came and had seen the grace of God, he was glad, and encouraged them all that with purpose of heart they should continue with the Lord (Acts 11:21-23).

This passage, and especially verse 23, is one of many exhortations used by Arminians in their effort to disprove eternal security. Their argument goes something like this: "Here you have Paul and Barnabas encouraging disciples to continue with the Lord. What would be the use of such an appeal if it wasn't possible for them to leave the Lord and thus be lost?" The argument is invalid. When we encourage young believers to go on for the Lord, we are not warning them against the loss of salvation. We're urging them to continue in the only life that really counts. That was the case with Paul and Barnabas. If the disciples continued with the Lord, they would enjoy the abundant life and find deliverance from tons of troubles. It is not a question of salvation but of discipleship.

...Strengthening the souls of the disciples, exhorting them to con-

tinue in the faith, and saying, "We must through many tribula-tions enter the kingdom of God" (Acts 14:22).

The kingdom of heaven has a past, present, and future tense. The past is when Jesus was on earth; the kingdom was present in the Person of the King (Mt. 12:28; Lk. 17:21). The kingdom at present is in mystery form; the King is absent but believers acknowledge Him as their rightful Ruler. In the future, the kingdom will be manifest; Christ will sit on His throne in Jerusalem and reign for 1,000 years. The kingdom on earth merges into the everlasting kingdom in heaven.

The only way to become a true citizen of the kingdom is to be born again (Jn. 3:3, 5). Tribulation is not the way of salvation, but it is what we encounter on the road to the future kingdom. It is promised to all believers.

In Jude's epistle, he gave his readers a similar encouragement:

But you, beloved, building yourselves up on your most holy faith, praying in the Holy Spirit, keep yourselves in the love of God, looking for the mercy of our Lord Jesus Christ unto eternal life (Jude 1:20-21).

When Jude exhorts us to keep ourselves in the love of God, he is not saying that we can or should keep ourselves saved. He is talking about fellowship, not relationship. We do this by spending time daily in the Word, praying in the Holy Spirit, confessing and forsaking all known sin, and living in the expectation of Christ's return.

Paul's concern for the Thessalonians' *continuation,* expressed in 1 Thessalonians 3, is sometimes mistaken for a concern about their *preservation:*

Therefore, when we could no longer endure it, we thought it good to be left in Athens alone, and sent Timothy, our brother and minister of God, and our fellow laborer in the gospel of Christ, to establish you and encourage you concerning your faith, that no one should be shaken by these afflictions; for you yourselves know that we are appointed to this. For, in fact, we told you before when we were with you that we would suffer tribulation, just as it happened, and you know. For this reason, when I could no longer endure it, I sent to know your faith, lest by some means the tempter had tempted you, and our labor might be in vain. But now that Timothy has come to us from you, and brought us good news of your faith and love, and that you always have good remembrance of us, greatly desiring to see us, as we also to see you—therefore, brethren, in all our affliction and distress we were comforted concerning you by your faith. For now we live, if you stand fast in the Lord (1 Thess. 3:1-8).

How does this passage support the falling away doctrine? Advocates of that doctrine use it this way: "Paul expresses concern that the Thessalonians stand fast in the Lord and in the faith. This implies the possibility that they might not do it and thus be eternally lost." But what are the facts?

The Thessalonians were suffering intense persecution because they were committed Christians. The apostle had led them to the Lord, had brought them up in the faith, and had warned them that tribulation would come. He did not want to see them cave in under their afflictions. They might give themselves over to discouragement and despair. And so he sent Timothy to strengthen and encourage them. Timothy brought back the good news that their faith had not wavered and that their love was undiminished, especially for Paul and his co-workers.

It was not at all a question of losing their faith but of their confidence becoming weakened and disillusioned by the fires of persecution.

Paul's great chapter on his desire to grow in the knowledge of Christ, Philippians 3, is sometimes taken as if even he were expressing concern that he might perhaps fall away:

2 Beware of dogs, beware of evil workers, beware of the mutilation! 3 For we are the circumcision, who worship God in the Spirit, rejoice in Christ Jesus, and have no confidence in the flesh, 4 though I also might have confidence in the flesh. If any-

119

*one else thinks he may have confidence in the flesh, I more so:
5 circumcised the eighth day, of the stock of Israel, of the tribe of
Benjamin, a Hebrew of the Hebrews; concerning the law, a
Pharisee; 6 concerning zeal, persecuting the church; concerning
the righteousness which is in the law, blameless. 7 But what
things were gain to me, these I have counted loss for Christ.
8 Yet indeed I also count all things loss for the excellence of the
knowledge of Christ Jesus my Lord, for whom I have suffered the
loss of all things, and count them as rubbish, that I may gain
Christ 9 and be found in Him, not having my own righteousness,
which is from the law, but that which is through faith in Christ,
the righteousness which is from God by faith; 10 that I may know
Him and the power of His resurrection, and the fellowship of His
sufferings, being conformed to His death, 11 if, by any means, I
may attain to the resurrection from the dead. 12 Not that I have
already attained, or am already perfected; but I press on, that I
may lay hold of that for which Christ Jesus has also laid hold of
me. 13 Brethren, I do not count myself to have apprehended; but
one thing I do, forgetting those things which are behind and
reaching forward to those things which are ahead, 14 I press toward the goal for the prize of the upward call of God in Christ
Jesus. 15 Therefore let us, as many as are mature, have this
mind; and if in anything you think otherwise, God will reveal
even this to you. 16 Nevertheless, to the degree that we have already attained, let us walk by the same rule, let us be of the same
mind. 17 Brethren, join in following my example, and note those
who so walk, as you have us for a pattern. 18 For many walk, of
whom I have told you often, and now tell you even weeping, that
they are the enemies of the cross of Christ: 19 whose end is destruction, whose god is their belly, and whose glory is in their
shame—who set their mind on earthly things. 20 For our citizen-
ship is in heaven, from which we also eagerly wait for the Savior, the Lord Jesus Christ, 21 who will transform our lowly body
that it may be conformed to His glorious body, according to the
working by which He is able even to subdue all things to Him-*

self. 1 *Therefore, my beloved and longed-for brethren, my joy and crown, so stand fast in the Lord, beloved* (Phil. 3:2-4:1).

Here we have another passage that is purported to prove conditional salvation. Let us see if that is what it really says.

In verses 5-6, Paul lists his excellent credentials in the areas of pedigree, orthodoxy, personal character, and zeal in service. But now that he is saved, he looks on any personal points of pride as rubbish compared with the privilege of knowing Christ Jesus his Lord. From now on, his boasting is that he is in Christ—not in his own righteousness, but that which was imputed to him by faith. Verse 9 cannot mean the apostle was struggling to be in Christ or that he was hoping for righteousness. These were facts in his life. But to obtain these incomparable blessings by faith, it was no great sacrifice to count all else but refuse and suffer the loss of all things.

Now his one unchanged ambition is to know Christ, the power of His resurrection, the fellowship of His suffering, conformity to His death, and resurrection from the dead.

To know Christ. He already knew Him, but wants to know Him in an ever deeper way. His prayer, in the words of a hymn, was:

> *Help me to serve Thee more and more,*
> *Help me to praise Thee o'er and o'er.*
> *Live in Thy presence day by day,*
> *Never to turn from Thee away.*
> —Author unknown

And the power of His resurrection. He wanted to know experientially some measure of the enormous power that raised the Lord Jesus from the tomb. In Ephesians 1:19-20, he piled words upon words in order to capture the immensity of that power.

Being conformed to His death. This may be understood figuratively or literally. If the former is taken, then it means that Paul would die daily in the service of Christ (1 Cor. 15:31). Or he may be saying, "Did the Lord Jesus die in fulfillment of God's will? Then that's what I want."

Sometimes he spoke of himself as among those who would go to heaven without dying (1 Thess. 4:17: "...we who are alive and remain shall be caught up together..."). At other times he wrote as if he would go to heaven by way of death (2 Tim. 4:6b: "...the time of my departure is at hand").

If, by any means, I may attain to the resurrection from the dead. This cannot possibly mean that Paul was uncertain that he would be raised at the Rapture. He was absolutely sure of that fact (1 Thess. 4:17; 1 Cor. 15:51). What he was saying was this: "I don't care what trials, perils, sufferings, and persecutions may lie between now and the resurrection. I'm willing to endure them all."

The word "resurrection" always refers to the body. It is the body that dies, and it is the body that will be raised. Here it is the resurrection *out from among* the dead ones.[1] It refers to Christ's coming for His saints. Only believers will be raised at that time.

The gist of Paul's words here is this: "Did Jesus die? Then I want to die! Did Jesus rise from the dead? Then I want to rise that way too!" It's as if he wanted to be so closely identified with his Lord that he didn't want to go to heaven in any more comfortable way.

In verse 11, he goes on to assure the Philippians that he didn't want them to think that he had achieved spiritual perfection. He had not "arrived" but he pressed on to see God's purpose fulfilled in his life. Like a swift runner, he gave his best in a life of service, not for salvation but for the rewarding crown. He encourages all believers to follow his example of high motivation and discipline.

The apostle denounces false teachers who show by their ungodly, earthly behavior that they are enemies of the cross of Christ (vv. 18-19). In striking contrast, true believers are citizens of heaven who wait for the coming of the Savior and for glorified bodies. Until that great event, they should stand fast in the Lord, allowing nothing to shake their confidence (4:1).

In the light of these passages, let us by all means "go on for the Lord" more and more. But we need not labor under the weight of the idea that we must keep ourselves from failing to persevere. That is the Lord's part of the job!

ENDNOTE

1 Paul uses a unique word here, not the usual word for resurrection, but, literally, "out-resurrection."

21
Occasional or Habitual?

There is a difference in the New Testament between committing acts of sin and practicing sin as a way of life. A Christian can and does sin, but he doesn't sin habitually. This distinction is brought out in 1 John 3:4-9 and 5:18, although most translations fail to show it by failing to use the continuous present tense of the verbs.

Whoever commits sin also commits lawlessness, and sin is lawlessness. And you know that He was manifested to take away our sins, and in Him there is no sin. Whoever abides in Him does not sin. Whoever sins has neither seen Him nor known Him. Little children, let no one deceive you. He who practices righteousness is righteous, just as He is righteous. He who sins is of the devil, for the devil has sinned from the beginning. For this purpose the Son of God was manifested, that He might destroy the works of the devil. Whoever has been born of God does not sin, for His seed remains in him; and he cannot sin, because he has been born of God...We know that whoever is born of God does not sin; but he who has been born of God keeps himself, and the wicked one does not touch him.

Before looking at these verses, let us take an overall view of what the Scriptures teach regarding the believer's relationship to sin.

First of all, God's will is that His people should not sin (1 Jn. 2:1). He cannot excuse or condone any amount of sin. His holiness demands that His opposition to sin should allow for no exceptions. God could not say, "My little children, sin as little as possible."

But the sad truth is that Christians *do* sin. Anyone who says he has no sin is self-deceived and void of the true facts (1 Jn. 1:8). And if he says he has not sinned, he is accusing God of lying and is ignorant of God's Word (1 Jn. 1:10). Christians who claim to be sinlessly perfect simply do not understand what sin is or have radically redefined the word!

Although we do sin, we must not say that we have to sin. That is not biblical language. We have the power of God at our call. In moments of temptation, we can call on the Lord to deliver us. He never fails (1 Cor. 10:13). The trouble is that we don't call on Him.

As we have seen, God's inflexible will for us is "Don't sin." But in grace, He has made provision for failure.

And if anyone sins, we have an Advocate with the Father, Jesus Christ the righteous. And He Himself is the propitiation for our sins, and not for ours only but also for the whole world (1 Jn. 2:1b-2).

Notice that it says "if," not "when." Sin should be considered exceptional rather than expectable or probable. Notice too that if anyone sins, we have an Advocate with the Father. Even when we sin, He is still our Father and we are still His children. This is convincing proof that sin does not break the relationship.

Our Advocate is Jesus Christ the righteous. His work is to restore His sinning saint to fellowship with the Father. He can do this righteously by pleading the value of the blood that He shed at Calvary. He is the propitiation for our sins, that is, His substitutionary sacrifice fully satisfies all the righteous claims of God against our sins. His work is *sufficient* for the sins of the whole world but *effective* only for those who accept Him as Lord and Savior.

It's obvious that a child of God can commit any sin against which a genuine believer is clearly warned in the New Testament. The potential for evil is staggering. And every sin breaks fellowship with God.

But the good news is that "if we confess our sins, He is faithful and just to forgive us our sins and to cleanse us from all unrighteousness" (1 Jn. 1:9). This is not the way of salvation for the unsaved, but the way of restoration for the believer. The unsaved person receives *judicial* forgiveness when he believes on the Lord Jesus Christ (Acts 16:31). The saint receives *parental* forgiveness when he confesses his sin (obviously with the intention of forsaking it; see Prov. 28:13). Judicial forgiveness means that the penalty of all the person's sins was paid by Christ on the Cross ("having forgiven you all trespasses" [Col. 2:13]), and he is now and forever free from condemnation (Rom. 8:1). Parental forgiveness means that the happy communion in the family of God is restored.

Now we come to the difference between acts and habit. Although a true Christian may commit acts of sin, he is not dominated by sin (Rom. 6:14). His life is not characterized by sin. Sin may be occasional but it is not habitual. The Living Bible succeeds in capturing the idea of continued practice:

> *But those who keep on sinning are against God, for every sin is done against the will of God. And you know that he became a man so that he could take away our sins, and that there is no sin in him, no missing of God's will at any time in any way. So if we stay close to him, obedient to him, we won't be sinning either; but as for those who keep on sinning, they should realize this: They sin because they have never really known him or become his. Oh, dear children, don't let anyone deceive you about this: if you are constantly doing what is good, it is because you are good, even as he is. But if you keep on sinning, it shows that you belong to Satan, who since he first began to sin has kept steadily at it. But the Son of God came to destroy these works of the devil. The person who has been born into God's family does not make a practice of sinning, because now God's life is in him; so he can't keep on sinning, for this new life has been born into him and controls him—he has been born again* (1 Jn. 3:4-9, TLB).

> *No one who has become part of God's family makes a practice of sinning, for Christ, God's Son, holds him securely and the devil cannot get his hands on him* (1 Jn. 5:18, TLB).

Gardiner Spring explains:

The children of God therefore do sin. They sin knowingly. They sin voluntarily, but they do not sin habitually. It is not the prevailing habit of their lives to disobey the commandments of God, but their purpose [is] to obey always and their practice to obey habitually. In forming our estimate of the fruits of righteousness, therefore, we are not to attribute too much importance to particular instances of conduct. The life of every good man is stained with imperfection and sin, and if we pronounce none good unless we find absolute perfection, all must be condemned. On the contrary, there is scarcely any bad man whose conduct does not sometimes exhibit the semblance of real goodness. We can say no more therefore of good men than that their obedience is habitual and that their conduct, viewed as a whole, exhibits clear and decisive evidences of a sanctified temper. This is most surely true of every Christian.[1]

That, of course leads to the question, "When do acts become habitual?" The Bible wisely does not answer the question. If it did, some Christians might be tempted to get as close to the edge as possible. God's silence warns them to stay as far away as possible.

Some extra-sensitive soul may worry that, because of a besetting sin, he is actually a habitual sinner. Here is one way in which he can decide. Let us say that he works in a business office. The other employees know that he is different. He doesn't laugh at dirty jokes, doesn't participate in their drinking parties, doesn't stoop to shady business deals. Then one day an unguarded word slips out of his mouth. Immediately they jump on him, saying, "We thought you were a Christian!" They know that characteristically he is a believer, but this is an aberration from his normal standard.

The real problem is with those who talk like Christians but live like the devil. They know all the right answers, they have "prayed the sinner's prayer," and they may well have been baptized. But their life is no different from that of their pagan neighbors. We have every reason to believe that they were never born again because there is no evidence of divine life. Profession of being a Christian is worthless if it does not result in a changed life.

It is possible for a believer to backslide. He can get very far from the Lord. Until he repents and confesses his waywardness, we are justified in doubting his profession. But if he is a true child of God, he will experience guilt, shame, and the discipline of God. He will learn that, although he may have eternal security, he can't sin and get away with it. God will chasten him sooner or later.

In spite of our finest efforts to decide whether people are counterfeit Christians or backsliders, we have to acknowledge that there are cases where only God knows. "The Lord knows those who are His" (2 Tim. 2:19). In the meantime, those who claim to be Christians should prove it by departing from iniquity.

ENDNOTE

1 Gardiner Spring, *The Distinguishing Traits of Christian Character,* Phillipsburg, N.J.: Presbyterian and Reformed Publishing Co., 1980, p. 72 (emphasis in original).

22
Reformation or Regeneration?

In studying the security of a believer, it's necessary to distinguish between reformation and regeneration. *Reformation* is turning over a new leaf; *regeneration* is receiving a new life. The former is an act of the will; the latter is an act of God. Reformation puts a new suit on the man; regeneration puts a new man in the suit. It's the difference between a New Year's resolution and a new birth.

There are two classic examples of reformation in the New Testament. The first is the story of a man out of whom an unclean spirit departed (Mt. 12:43-45; Lk. 11:24-26). When the spirit returned, he found the home empty, swept, and put in order. So he rounded up seven more evil spirits and took possession of the house with the result that the man was worse off than ever.

As to the interpretation, the passage deals primarily with the nation of Israel ("this wicked generation," Mt. 12:45). The Babylonian captivity delivered the people from the worship of graven images. In that sense, the house had been cleaned. But the house was left unoccupied; the nation refused to admit the Messiah. As a result, Israel will yet be guilty of a worse form of idolatry, that is, the worship of the Antichrist. Reformation was not enough. Without the Messiah, there is no final deliverance from evil.

The second illustration of reformation is found in 2 Peter 2.

For when they speak great swelling words of emptiness, they allure through the lusts of the flesh, through lewdness, the ones who have actually escaped from those who live in error. While they promise them liberty, they themselves are slaves of corruption; for by whom a person is overcome, by him also he is brought into bondage. For if, after they have escaped the pollu-

tions of the world through the knowledge of the Lord and Savior Jesus Christ, they are again entangled in them and overcome, the latter end is worse for them than the beginning. For it would have been better for them not to have known the way of righteousness, than having known it, to turn from the holy commandment delivered to them. But it has happened to them according to the true proverb: "A dog returns to his own vomit," and, "a sow, having washed, to her wallowing in the mire" (2 Pet. 2:18-22).

The passage tells of people who have been living in sin but who decide they want to clean up their act. So they go to their local cleric for advice. But instead of telling them how to be born again, this false teacher condones their sin, boasts that he himself engages in it, and encourages them to give full expression to their natural appetites.

They knew what was right, but rejected that knowledge with the result that they sink lower than ever in a life of shame and degradation. They are like a dog that returns to its vomit and a sow that goes back to wallowing in the mud. Both the dog and pig were unclean animals in the Old Testament. Their nature is unclean and their behavior is unclean. So it was with these people. Although they had reformed, they had never received a new nature. The dog was still a canine and the sow was still a swine.

What sinful people need is regeneration. This is a marvelous, mysterious, miraculous work of the Spirit of God which takes place when a sinner repents and acknowledges Jesus Christ as his Lord and Savior. It is likened to a bath in Titus 3:5. The instrument of the new birth is the Word of God (1 Pet. 1:23).

It is a *new* birth (Jn. 3:3, 5). The person becomes a child of God (Jn. 1:12-13). Once a birth takes place, it is forever. Nothing can ever undo it.[1] I was born a son of William and Jessie MacDonald. I might bring shame on them, disown them, and in some ridiculous legal jurisdictions even "divorce" them. But the stubborn fact remains: I am still their son. They will always be my parents.

Going back to the illustration of the dog and the sow, these un-

132

clean animals never became sheep, i.e. clean animals. When anyone is regenerated, he becomes a sheep of Christ. And because of that, he will never perish (Jn. 10:28). It's a birth that can never be undone.

There's a difference between a nominal Christian and a real one. When anyone is born again, he becomes a new creation in Christ Jesus. He experiences a new life, the life of Christ in him. No question about it. The Lord Jesus makes a difference when He comes. A person whose life is what it always has been is not a Christian. The believer has new loves, new motives, new ambitions, and a new lifestyle. Let us list some of the things that characterize a child of God.

He disclaims any personal merit. If you ask him if he is saved, he is apt to answer, "Yes, but only by the grace of God."

He has a new love for God (1 Jn. 5:2). Before conversion, he was hostile to the Lord, or was indifferent to Him, or tolerated Him, or feared Him. But now he instinctively calls Him "Father" (Gal. 4:6). The change is unmistakable.

He has a holy determination to make restitution for the wrongs of the past—for thefts, lies, law-breaking, and other wrongs (Lk. 19:8).

And he senses an inner compulsion to confess the Savior before his relatives and friends (Rom. 10:9). Naturally speaking he might be a very timid person, but he is driven to proclaim the Lord Jesus. In obedience to Christ, he confesses Him by being baptized.

Prayer becomes as vital a part of life as the air line to a deep sea diver (Gal. 4:6; 1 Jn. 5:14-15; Acts 9:11). Even without being taught, he realizes the necessity of talking to his God and Father.

And the Bible finds a place in his life that it never had before. What food is to his body, so the Bible is to his soul (Ps. 119:162; 1 Pet. 2:2). In the Scriptures, he hears his Father speaking to him and he wants nothing more than to obey (1 Jn. 2:3-6, 17; 5:2; Jn. 14:15).

Soon he decides that *he must get rid of the paraphernalia* of his old life (Acts 19:19). It may be addictive chemicals, pornographic materials, questionable music, occult equipment—they all must go.

Because he loves the Lord, *he wants to serve Him.* He is driven by the mercies of God, the love of Christ, the shortness of time, and the fear of wasting his life on trivia.

He has a new love for Christians (1 Jn. 3:11, 14; 5:1). Before he knew the Lord, he may have looked down on them as odd and out of touch with reality. Now they are "his people," "the excellent of the earth in whom is all [his] delight" (Ps. 16:3).

He has a new love for the world of lost humanity (Rom. 1:14; Acts 4:20). As he begins to see others as people for whom Christ died, he becomes aware of an awesome sense of obligation to win them for the Savior. Even if they are unlovely, yes, and even if they manifest deep hatred, he yearns for their eternal welfare.

Nowhere is the change in a new believer's life more apparent than in his relationship to sin. Although he still commits acts of sin, *he is no longer a slave of sin.* Sin does not have dominion over him (Rom. 6:14). He is not sinless but he does sin less. He is freed from the practice of sin (1 Jn. 5:18).

Every true believer has an inborn love for holiness and an inborn hatred of sin (1 Jn. 3:8-9; Ps. 97:10). He can no longer sin and be comfortable. When he does sin, he has deeper guilt and conviction than he ever had before (Rom. 7:14-25). Now he realizes that he is sinning against grace. He is not only breaking the law of God; he is breaking His heart. And so he is in a hurry to confess his sin and appropriate his Father's forgiveness.

With the passing of time, other evidences of the new life appear. He practices righteousness (1 Jn. 2:29; 1 Jn. 3:7, 10). He now has a tenderized conscience that refuses to cheat, lie, steal, or engage in unethical practices. The fruit of the Spirit manifests itself—love, joy, peace, longsuffering, kindness, goodness, faithfulness, gentleness, and self-control (Gal. 5:22-23). He addicts himself to good works so that he might adorn the doctrine of God his Savior (Eph. 2:10; Jas. 2:14-26; Titus 2:7-10).

Increasingly he realizes that the world system is opposed to Christ and to Christian values (Jn. 15:18). He can no longer feel at home at worldly parties or at gatherings where the name of Christ is banned. He is *in the world* as a witness for Christ, but not *of the world* in its lusts and pride (Jn. 17:16). He finds himself moving to a life of separation to God from the world (1 Jn. 2:15-17).

One of the marks of new life that a newborn child of God realizes is that *he is no longer afraid to die.* He might not relish the thought of a painful death, but dying holds no terror for him.

Someone reading this might think that this is a heavy load to put on a new believer. But that misses the point. These are ways in which the life of Christ reveals itself in a person who has been genuinely converted. He does not do these things by his own strength. That would be too much. He is empowered by the Holy Spirit. While it is true that the person's own cooperation is involved, that is secondary. The real driving power is the Indwelling Christ.

ENDNOTE

1 Someone might ask, "Well, what about children of the devil (Jn. 8:44)? Are they doomed to remain in that relationship? Can't they be saved? The answer is that people don't become children of the devil by a birth but rather by imitating his behavior.

23
Condition or Criterion?

Some of the "if" clauses in the New Testament are grist for the mills of those who teach conditional salvation. They quote these clauses as if they were indisputable proof that our final salvation depends on our enduring, standing firm, continuing in the faith, or holding fast.

They forget that these "iffy" clauses are a criterion or characteristic of saved people rather than a condition of salvation. These describe traits of all who have been born again. Let us look at two passages in particular.

Moreover, brethren, I declare to you the gospel which I preached to you, which also you received and in which you stand, by which also you are saved, if you hold fast that word which I preached to you—unless you believed in vain (1 Cor. 15:1-2).

The Corinthians were truly saved if they held fast the gospel Paul preached to them—a gospel that included the resurrection. Otherwise they had believed in vain.

But why did he say this to those who were already Christians? Because he knew that there were some in the assembly whose salvation was questionable. Some even went so far as to deny the resurrection of Christ. It is to them he is saying, "You are saved by believing the true gospel, but if you are really saved, you will show it by holding fast the word I preached to you." Holding fast is the fruit of the new life, not a means of holding onto it. There is only one true gospel (vv. 2-4). To believe any other way of salvation is to believe in vain. Leave out the resurrection, as some were doing, and your faith is futile and you are still in your sins (v. 17).

It can't be emphasized too strongly that the moment you make ultimate salvation depend in part on something meritorious that you must do, you deny that you are saved by grace. Grace is a gift, not a debt. It is an unconditional covenant, telling what God will do, not what you must do.

Unless God does all the saving, we can never be sure of heaven because in ourselves we are weak, sinful, and unworthy. Even if God took us to the gate of heaven, and told us that we must cross the threshold by our own strength or virtue, we would never make it.

If it be argued (correctly) that the verb "saved" in verse 2 is in the present tense and may mean "are being saved," it does not change the conclusion.

As has already been mentioned, salvation has three tenses—past, present, and future. We *were saved* from the penalty of sins. We *are being saved* from the power of sin. We *shall be saved* from the presence of sin. The first is justification, the second is sanctification, and the third is glorification.

Paul is telling the Corinthians that if the message they believed and were still believing did not include the resurrection of Christ, they had believed in vain. But it's impossible to believe the true gospel in vain.

Some proponents of the "falling away" view treat salvation as conditional on our suffering in this life, based on Romans 8:17:

> ...*And if children, then heirs—heirs of God and joint heirs with Christ, if indeed we suffer with Him, that we may also be glorified together.*

In Romans 8, Paul distinguishes between believers and nonbelievers on the basis of their relationship to the Holy Spirit. He is *not* contrasting spiritual and unspiritual members of Christ's body. This is seen in the following chart:

138

	NONBELIEVERS	BELIEVERS
Verse 5	Those who live according to the flesh	Those who live according to the Spirit
Verse 6	Those who are carnally minded	Those who are spiritually minded
Verses 8-9	Those who are in the flesh	Those who are in the Spirit
Verses 9-10	Those who do not have the Spirit of Christ	Those who have Christ in them
Verse 13	Those who live according to the flesh	Those who by the Spirit put to death the deeds of the body
Verse 14		Those who are led by the Spirit of God
Verse 15	Those who have the spirit of bondage to fear	Those who have received the Spirit of adoption
Verse 17		Children of God, heirs of God, joint heirs with Christ

When the apostle says in verse 17, "...if indeed we suffer with Him, that we may be glorified together," he is not describing an elite inner circle of Christians but all the children of God. Two things are certain for all—suffering and glory. All who are justified will be glorified (Rom. 8:30c) but suffering comes before the glory. In the verses that follow he reminds us that everyone suffers; the whole creation "groans and labors with birth pangs until now." "We...who have the firstfruits of the Spirit...groan within ourselves." All God's children suffer.

Another "if" clause used by Arminians is Colossians 1:23:

...If indeed you continue in the faith, grounded and steadfast, and are not moved away from the hope of the gospel which you heard, which was preached to every creature under heaven, of which I, Paul, became a minister.

Here the question centers on the words "if indeed you continue in the faith...." Does this mean that our final salvation depends on our faithful continuance, not moving away from the hope of the gospel? Or is the thought that we demonstrate that our faith is genuine by this kind of track record?

The first explanation means that we can earn or lose our salvation by our own performance. But this is not the gospel of grace. We are not saved by anything meritorious that we can do. By His work on the Cross, Christ provides full, free, and eternal salvation quite apart from any merit on our part. In fact, it is in spite of our demerit.

The second explanation is the correct one. A true child of God continues in the faith, not in order to hold on to his salvation, but as a fruit of the new life. It is not a work of merit, but the outworking of the life of Christ within him. It is a matter of criterion, not of condition. So the passage is good for nominal Christians as well as genuine ones. It brings the former up short, causing them to realize their need of a real work of grace. And it encourages true children of God to press on toward the mark for the prize. Arthur Pridham says it well:

The reader will find, on a careful study of the Word, that it is the habit of the Spirit to accompany the fullest and most absolute statements of grace by warnings which imply a ruinous failure on the part of some who nominally stand in faith...Warnings which grate harshly on the ears of insincere profession are drunk willingly as medicine by the godly soul...The aim of all such teaching is to encourage faith, and condemn, by anticipation, reckless and confident professors.[1]

Or, as another has said, "These 'ifs' in Scripture look on professing Christians here in the world, and they come as healthy tests to the soul."

ENDNOTE

1 Further documentation unavailable.

24
Temporal Deliverance or Eternal Salvation?

Those who seek to disprove eternal security sometimes fail to realize that the word *save* and related words have a variety of meanings.

Save describes Christ's work in saving people from their sins. In this case, He delivers from eternal damnation. This is the aspect of salvation with which we are most familiar, and we tend to import this meaning whenever we find the word.

But salvation can also mean release from prison (Phil. 1:19), rescue from drowning (Acts 27:30-31), deliverance from danger (Mt. 8:25) and from sickness (Mt. 9:22)—in short, deliverance from almost any adverse situations of life.

Another important meaning of the word *save* is deliverance from spiritual damage in this life. Take 1 Timothy 4:16, for instance:

Take heed to yourself and to the doctrine. Continue in them, for in doing this you will save both yourself and those who hear you.

It should be clear at the outset that this can't mean soul salvation. Timothy couldn't even save himself from the wrath of God and certainly couldn't save others. But by taking heed to himself and by continuing in sound doctrine, he could avoid spiritual pitfalls and could save those to whom he ministered from errors and moral lapses.

Another example of this usage is James 1:21:

Therefore lay aside all filthiness and overflow of wickedness, and receive with meekness the implanted word, which is able to save your souls.

James is writing to believers. He's not telling them how to be saved from hell. They already are. But he's exhorting them to be done with the lifestyle that characterized them in their pre-conversion days. And he's urging them to obey the Word of God and thus save themselves from a heap of troubles.

It's true that the Word is the instrument which God uses in saving our souls from eternal damnation, but that is not the subject here. James is discussing sanctification, not regeneration. The subject is the present tense of salvation, that is, deliverance from the power of sin in a believer's life. Profound subjection to God's Word saves a person from the inevitable consequences of being out of fellowship with the Lord.

The expression "save your souls" never means to save from hell. Rather the thought is to save your lives from waste and ruin.

This is also the thought in James 5:19-20:

Brethren, if anyone among you wanders from the truth, and someone turns him back, let him know that he who turns a sinner from the error of his way will save a soul from death and cover a multitude of sins.

Here is the case of a backslider, a person who has wandered from the truth. He is no longer walking with the Lord. He has strayed from the path of duty. A Christian brother or sister engages in a restorative ministry with him and succeeds in turning him from the error of his ways.

Two dramatic results follow. First, the shepherd saves a soul from death. Here, as so often in Jewish usage, *soul* is used as a synonym for person. But how does he save a person from death? It cannot mean eternal death because that is achieved only by repentance toward God and faith in the Lord Jesus Christ. There is no mention of the gospel here. How then does he save the sinning saint from death? By turning him back from the error of his way. If James had meant eternal salvation, then that would be salvation by reformation, which is utterly contrary to the gospel of grace.

That leaves the question, "What is meant by *death*?" It is the living death, an existence of misery, guilt, and restlessness that goes with backsliding. David described it vividly in Psalm 32.

When I kept silent, my bones grew old through my groaning all the day long. For day and night Your hand was heavy upon me; my vitality was turned into the drought of summer (Ps. 32:3-4).

Of course, in this passage *death* could also refer to God's judgment on a believer who goes on in unconfessed sin (1 Cor. 11:30). But that is exceptional, whereas the above explanation is inescapable.

A related meaning of *salvation* deals with deliverance from problems in this life. Take Philippians 2:12, for example:

Therefore, my beloved, as you have always obeyed, not as in my presence only, but now much more in my absence, work out your own salvation with fear and trembling....

There is a definite flow of thought in this chapter, and in order to understand verse 12, we must trace this continuity:

There was a problem in the assembly at Philippi; some of the believers weren't getting along with one another (vv. 1-2; see also 4:2).

The way to handle this problem is to think of others, not of self: Esteem others better than self (v. 3b); look out for the interests of others (v. 4b). The key word is *others*.

The Lord Jesus is the prime example of One who lived for others; we should follow His example (v. 5). He humbled Himself to the extent of dying for others on the Cross (vv. 6-8).

God honored Him with the Name that is above every name, and with the promise of universal dominion (vv. 9-11).

It is at this point that Paul says, "Therefore, my beloved...work out your own salvation with fear and trembling" (v. 12). In other words, I have diagnosed your problem. I have given the solution.

145

Now work out the solution of your problem with a reverential fear of displeasing the Lord. In this verse salvation means temporal deliverance from the problem of disunity in the church. It has nothing to do with the salvation of the soul.

I admit that this is not the most common interpretation of the verse. Usually Christians explain it as meaning this: When God saves you, He puts eternal life in you, but then you are to work it out in lives of practical holiness. But it seems to me that this introduces a thought foreign to the context. The apostle has not been talking about the eternal salvation of the soul. Furthermore, in the original language of the New Testament, the word for "work out" is hardly ever used with this meaning. It always means, "work to accomplish."

But that leaves the question, "Why do proponents of the conditional salvation view use Philippians 2:12 to bolster their case?" One of the leading advocates explains it this way. "The command 'work out your own salvation' shows that man has a responsibility with his salvation." The initiative doesn't rest entirely with God. The presumption seems to be that if man doesn't do his part, he would lose his salvation.

This is an example of what happens when we fail to distinguish between temporal deliverance and eternal salvation.

Another example is found in 1 Timothy 2:15:

Nevertheless she will be saved in childbearing if they continue in faith, love, and holiness, with self-control.

We should mention at the outset that there are several different interpretations of the verse in Christian circles.

Some see it as a promise of a safe childbirth if the parents live as believers should. The trouble with this view is that many godly Christian women have had miscarriages and stillbirths, and many mothers, especially in the past, *have* died due to childbirth.

Some link it with the birth of the Lord Jesus who is our Savior. But since *all* believers are saved through Him, it seems too obvious to single out mothers.

146

Others suggest that a woman is saved from the corruption of society if she is a mother and home-keeper. There is a measure of truth in this.

In order to reach one other interpretation, we again appeal to the context. Paul is giving instructions about public worship. Prayer in meetings of the assembly is the ministry of the men, i.e. males.[1] Women are to dress modestly, learn in silence, refrain from teaching men, avoid exercising authority over a man, and learn in silence. To show that this was not a cultural matter, Paul goes back to the order in creation—Adam first, then Eve. And he goes back to the headship of man. Eve violated this by failing to consult her husband. She was deceived and brought untold consequences of sin into the world.

Now all this might create the impression that woman is reduced to a non-person. She has no worthwhile position in the church. Not so, says the apostle. She has the privilege of raising up godly seed for the ongoing of the church. Who is to say that this role is not more important than the male's? Isn't it true that the hand that rocks the cradle rules the world?

So the verse about a woman being saved in childbearing could clearly be speaking about *the salvation of her position in the church*. The role of motherhood saves her from thinking she is of no consequence. She is of *crucial* importance!

But there is a condition attached: "...if they [mothers] continue in faith, love, and holiness, with self-control." Her ability to raise godly children and spiritual leaders for the church depends in large measure on her serving as a proper role model.

It should be clear that this conditional clause does not refer to eternal salvation. Rather it deals with deliverance from any idea of a woman's being left without an important role in the church. Furthermore, the idea of childbearing as a means of soul salvation is bizarre, and totally opposed to salvation by grace, through faith, and apart from works.

147

ENDNOTE

1 In verse 8, Paul specifically uses a Greek word meaning "males" (*andres*, cf. *polyandry*, "many husbands"), not the word for human beings (*anthrōpoi*, cf. *anthropology*).

25
Literal Death or Figurative Death?

If we understand the different kinds of death that are found in the New Testament, it will help us understand verses that might seem to support conditional salvation.

First of all, there is *physical death,* the separation of the spirit and the body. James says, "...the body without the spirit is dead." Here death refers to the body but not to the spirit. The spirit is immortal.

Then there is *spiritual death.* Unsaved people are dead in trespasses and sins (Eph. 2:1, 5). This does not mean that their spirits are dead. It means that they are dead toward God.

Eternal death is also called *the second death* (Rev. 20:14). It is the destiny of all unbelievers in the lake of fire.

And *death* can be used as a figure of speech to describe a backslider. It means that a believer has grown cold. He is spiritually unresponsive, and lacking in spiritual activity.

This was the case with the saints in the church at Sardis. The Lord said to them, "I know your works, that you have a name that you are alive, but you are dead" (Rev. 3:1). They were physically and spiritually alive, but as far as their works were concerned, they were dead. Note: "I know your works...you are dead." And again in verse 2, "...I have not found your works perfect before God."

We have a similar use of the word *dead* in 1 Timothy 5:3-6.

Honor widows who are really widows. But if any widow has children or grandchildren, let them first learn to show piety at home and to repay their parents; for this is good and acceptable before God. Now she who is really a widow, and left alone, trusts in

God and continues in supplications and prayers night and day. But she who lives in pleasure is dead while she lives.

It may be, of course, that the widow of verse 6 is only a nominal Christian. But that is not necessarily so. Paul is contrasting her with a widow who trusts in God and continues in supplications and prayers night and day. The widow of verse 6 is dead to that kind of a life. She lives in pleasure. Perhaps she is like those in verse 11: "When their sensual desires overcome their dedication to Christ, they want to marry" (NIV). In her obsession to find a husband, she forgets her household duties, neglects the Bible and prayer, gads about, and becomes a busybody. To outward appearances, she is dead to her first faith.

26
Reward or Ruin?

In His marvelous plan of redemption, God has linked

faith → salvation
works → reward

Rewards are earned. Salvation is not.

By failing to remember this, advocates of the falling away doctrine have drawn false conclusions. For instance, they quote 1 Corinthians 9:24-27 in an attempt to prove that Paul could have become disqualified[1] for heaven:

Do you not know that those who run in a race all run, but one receives the prize? Run in such a way that you may obtain it. And everyone who competes for the prize is temperate in all things. Now they do it to obtain a perishable crown, but we for an imperishable crown. Therefore I run thus: not with uncertainty. Thus I fight: not as one who beats the air. But I discipline my body and bring it into subjection, lest, when I have preached to others, I myself should become disqualified.

Notice the apostle's references to "prize" and "crown" (vv. 24-25). These make it clear that the context is service and reward. Paul runs in his life of service with single-mindedness, concentration, and discipline so that he will win an imperishable crown. Without giving it all he has, he realizes that he might be disqualified as a servant of the Lord. He cannot mean disqualified for heaven because the believer's fitness for heaven is found in Christ and not in himself. It is in Christ we are accepted (Eph. 1:6). In Him we are complete (Col. 2:10). But we can be relegated to the sidelines as far as

151

service is concerned by not observing the training regulations and the rules of the race.

A second passage used to support the conditional security view is Galatians 6:7-9:

Do not be deceived, God is not mocked; for whatever a man sows, that he will also reap. For he who sows to his flesh will of the flesh reap corruption, but he who sows to the Spirit will of the Spirit reap everlasting life. And let us not grow weary in doing good, for in due season we shall reap if we do not lose heart.

These verses clearly have to do with our stewardship of money and other material things. It encourages us to be generous and to do as much good as possible. When Paul says, "...whatever a man sows, that he will also reap," he is not thinking of sins and eternal punishment (although that is *also* true). Rather he is concerned with what we do with our *money.*

The one who sows to the flesh is the Christian who uses his material resources for self-indulgence. He caters to the body. At the end of his life, the body he lived for will return to dust. He has a harvest of corruption.

The one who sows to the Spirit is the believer who is a faithful steward, living sacrificially for the spread of the gospel. He reaps eternal life through the ministry of the Spirit. But does this mean that he buys eternal life with his dollars? It can't mean that. Salvation can't be purchased, earned, or deserved. But the one who generously supports the Lord's work and workers reaps a harvest of fuller enjoyment of eternal life, greater rewards in heaven, and a greater capacity for enjoying heaven.

There is always an interval between sowing and harvest, so we should be tireless in doing good, assured that eventually we will be rewarded.

Here is another passage mistakenly taken to refer to salvation:

Brethren, I do not count myself to have apprehended; but one thing I do, forgetting those things which are behind and reaching forward to those things which are ahead, I press toward the goal for the prize of the upward call of God in Christ Jesus (Phil. 3:13-14).

Again the apostle likens himself to an athlete in a race. The goal is conformity to Christ (vv. 10-11). He has not yet reached it, but with singleness of purpose ("one thing I do") he presses on toward the goal for the prize. "The upward call of God in Christ Jesus" is the fulfillment of the purposes God had in mind in saving him.

It does violence to the passage to see it as teaching salvation as a reward for running a faithful race. Salvation is not a prize to be won, but a gift to be accepted.

Next we turn to Colossians 2:18-19, verses that supposedly teach that salvation can be forfeited:

Let no one cheat you of your reward, taking delight in false humility and worship of angels, intruding into those things which he has not seen, vainly puffed up by his fleshly mind, and not holding fast to the Head, from whom all the body, nourished and knit together by joints and ligaments, grows with the increase that is from God.

The word *reward* in verse 18 should alert us to the fact that salvation is not in view. It's not a question of losing one's salvation, but of losing out on one's reward. Paul is warning the Colossians against unscriptural novelties. Preoccupation with legalism, mysticism, or asceticism turns one's attention away from Christ, the Head, who is the source of spiritual growth. Christians who get sidetracked in this way are stunted in their growth and cheated of their reward.

But also for this very reason, giving all diligence, add to your faith virtue, to virtue knowledge, to knowledge self-control, to self-control perseverance, to perseverance godliness, to godliness brotherly kindness, and to brotherly kindness love. For if these things are yours and abound, you will be neither barren nor unfruitful in the knowledge of our Lord Jesus Christ. For he who lacks these things is shortsighted, even to blindness, and has forgotten that he was cleansed from his old sins. Therefore, brethren, be even more diligent to make your call and election sure, for if you do these things you will never stumble; for so an entrance will be supplied to you abundantly into the everlasting kingdom of our Lord and Savior Jesus Christ (2 Pet. 1:5-11).

Verses 10 and 11 are the ones that are alleged to support conditional salvation, but first let's examine the Scriptures that lead up to them. Verses 5-7 are an exhortation to the development of Christian character. As we develop these graces in our lives, we are saved from barrenness, unfruitfulness, shortsightedness, and forgetfulness of what we've been saved from.

With that background, Peter urges us to make our calling and election sure. In one sense, they are as sure as God can make them. We were chosen in Christ before the foundation of the world (Eph. 1:4), and called by the gospel to belong to Him. But by the development of mature spiritual character, we demonstrate to ourselves and especially to others the reality of our election and call. It is a visible confirmation. And this spiritual growth will save us from stumbling. Here it is not a question of losing one's salvation, but of taking a spiritual tumble, from which there can of course be recovery.

We must be careful to read verse 11 accurately. It does *not* say, "For so an entrance will be supplied to you into the everlasting kingdom...." Don't leave out the word "abundantly!" We enter the kingdom by being born again (Jn. 3:5). But the abundance of our entrance is determined by the extent to which we develop the Christian graces in our lives. Peter is not speaking about the way of salvation but rather about the rewards of a godly life. He wants us to enter God's realm with all flags flying!

It's surprising that those who believe a person can lose his salvation would use 2 John 1:8.

Look to yourselves, that we do not lose those things we worked for, but that we may receive a full reward.

154

According to this translation, John is saying, "You Christians, look to yourselves, that we (the apostles) do not lose those things we worked for, but that we may receive a full reward."

The New International Version, following the Nestle-United Bible Societies' Greek text, reads, "Watch out that you do not lose what you have worked for, but that you may be rewarded fully."

In either case, it's not a question of losing salvation. We don't work for that. It's a question of gaining a full reward.

Here are some other passages that those who deny eternal security use to combat it. The first is Revelation 2:10-11:

Do not fear any of those things which you are about to suffer. Indeed, the devil is about to throw some of you into prison, that you may be tested, and you will have tribulation ten days. Be faithful until death, and I will give you the crown of life. He who has an ear, let him hear what the Spirit says to the churches. He who overcomes shall not be hurt by the second death.

In verse 10, the crown of life is promised those who are faithful until death. Our "falling away" friends make the crown of life synonymous with eternal life, and it is for those who continue to believe to the end of their lives. That is the argument.

But we appeal to the *context* for the true meaning. The first part of the verse speaks of the terrible suffering that the saints in Smyrna would endure. They would face prison, testing, and tribulation. Some would even have to die for the faith. To them would be given the martyr's crown—the crown of life.

In verse 11, the Lord promises that the overcomer will not be hurt by the second death. Advocates of conditional salvation allege that means one who believes and continues to believe, who overcomes and continues to overcome. The apostle John says that it means one who believes that Jesus is the Son of God (1 Jn. 5:5). (This is dealt with more fully in the next chapter.) The second death is the doom of unbelievers only.

Now we consider a final passage where salvation and rewards are often confused:

I know your works. See, I have set before you an open door, and no one can shut it; for you have a little strength, have kept My word, and have not denied My name. Indeed I will make those of the synagogue of Satan, who say they are Jews and are not, but lie—indeed I will make them come and worship before your feet, and to know that I have loved you. Because you have kept My command to persevere, I also will keep you from the hour of trial which shall come upon the whole world, to test those who dwell on the earth. Behold, I am coming quickly! Hold fast what you have, that no one may take your crown. He who overcomes, I will make him a pillar in the temple of My God, and he shall go out no more. I will write on him the name of My God and the name of the city of My God, the New Jerusalem, which comes down from heaven from My God. And I will write on him My new name (Rev. 3:8-12).

The word "works" at the beginning of verse 8 signals us that John is speaking about rewards. Philadelphia's reward for keeping Christ's Word and not denying His name would be to have their enemies bow before their feet and realize that the saints were loved by Him. Because they had kept His command to persevere, He will keep them from the Tribulation period. Until He comes, they should hold fast what they had so that no one could take their crown (not their salvation but their *crown*). The reward for overcoming will be to be made pillars in the temple of God. And on them will be written the name of God, the name of the City of God, the name of the New Jerusalem, and Christ's new name.

All these honors are for faithfulness in life and service but are not means of obtaining salvation. Works that endure will be rewarded. Other works will be burned up and the servant will suffer loss, but he himself will be saved (1 Cor. 3:14-15).

ENDNOTE

1 The KJV here, "castaway," is especially unfortunate since today it sounds like "falling away." It's really an athletic term, "not approved" or "disqualified."

27
Overcomers or Shortcomers?

One of the troubling verses in connection with the question of eternal security is Revelation 3:5:

He who overcomes shall be clothed in white garments, and I will not blot out his name from the Book of Life; but I will confess his name before My Father and before His angels.

The words "I will not blot his name from the Book of Life" seem to imply the possibility that those who don't overcome *will* be blotted out. At the outset, this raises two questions: "What is an overcomer?" and "What is the Book of Life?"

The basic definition of an overcomer is found in 1 John 5:4-5: he is one who overcomes the world.

For whatever is born of God overcomes the world. And this is the victory that has overcome the world—our faith. Who is he who overcomes the world, but he who believes that Jesus is the Son of God?

In these verses, overcomers are those who are born of God, those who believe that Jesus is the Son of God—in other words, genuine Christians.

These verses in 1 John 5 are sometimes used to support the conditional view. I see nothing here to substantiate this unless its supporters appeal to the present tense of the word "believe" and insist that it means continuous action. In other words, the one who overcomes the world must believe and keep on believing. And it necessarily follows that a person is only born of God as long as he persists in believing.[1]

According to this, a person can be born of God, then he can become unborn (a bizarre idea), and then he can be spiritually reborn again. There is apparently no limit to the number of times this cycle can be repeated. It is as if the Scriptures taught, "You must be born again, and again, and again, and again." The Bible knows nothing of this.

What the verses *do* teach is that faith enables the born-again believer to overcome the world by seeing through its glitter and emptiness, by realizing it is at enmity with God and His people, and by fearing its flattery but not its frown. He doesn't expect to be treated better than his Lord was.

A genuine saint does continue to believe, not as a condition of salvation, but as a feature of his new life. Three times the apostle John addresses young men in the family of God as those who have overcome the evil one (1 Jn. 2:13-14; 4:4a). But they didn't do it in their own strength, but by the power of the One who indwells them (1 Jn. 4:4b).

We now return to our original verse in Revelation. Notice the promises that are made to an overcomer, here and elsewhere in the book: He will eat from the tree of life (2:7). He will not be hurt by the second death (2:11). (Since the second death is the lake of fire and since only unbelievers will be hurt by the second death [Rev. 20:14], every overcomer is a true child of God.) He will eat of the hidden manna (2:17). He will be given power over the nations (2:26). He will be clothed in white garments (3:5a). He will be a pillar in the temple of God (3:12). He will sit with Christ on His throne (3:21). He will inherit all things, God will be his Father, and he will be God's son (21:7).

Taking all these passages together, we not only learn that all overcomers are believers, but also that all believers are looked on as overcomers.

John MacArthur explains: "'He that overcometh,' and parallel expressions, are common in John's writings. The apostle John quite plainly uses the concept of the 'overcomer' as a synonym for the believer. By his definition, all Christians are ultimately 'overcomers'.... There is therefore no such thing as a believer who is not an overcomer in this sense."[2]

Now let's consider the Book of Life. The names of Paul's fellow workers are in the Book of Life (Phil. 4:3). The names of those who worship the beast from the sea have not been written in the Book of Life of the Lamb (Rev. 13:8). Those not registered in the Book of Life are cast into the lake of fire (Rev. 20:15). Only those whose names are written in the Lamb's Book of Life will enter the New Jerusalem (Rev. 21:27).

Taking these all together, it is apparent that the Book of Life is a register of all the redeemed. (In some Bible versions, the Book of Life is mentioned in Revelation 22:19, but the most authentic manuscripts have "tree of life" in this verse.)

So now we come back to the basic problem: The Lord says in Revelation 3:5 that He will not blot out the names of overcomers from the Book of Life. Doesn't this imply that the names of some believers could be blotted out?

First of all, we must not build a doctrine on *what might seem to be implied.* Better to take direct statements.

Then we should know that the opposite of a statement is not necessarily implied nor true. For instance, I might say, "If I'm in Jerusalem, then I know I'm in Israel." The converse would be, "If I'm not in Jerusalem, then I know I'm not in Israel." That's not true. You might be in Haifa or Tel Aviv.

Actually the Lord's promise that He wouldn't blot out the names of believers is a promise of their eternal security. If He does not blot them out, then they remain in the Book of Life. Instead of taking His words to imply an ominous possibility, it is better to take them as a positive statement of what He will not do.

And they overcame him by the blood of the Lamb and by the word of their testimony, and they did not love their lives to the death (Rev. 12:11).

This describes saints of the Tribulation period who had been threatened with death if they did not recant their faith in Christ.

They had overcome the devil by the blood of the Lamb. The shed blood of Christ met every charge that Satan could bring against them. And they had overcome by the word of their testimony: They would not retract their confession of Christ, even if it meant dying as martyrs. "They did not love their lives to the death." It is hard to see how this verse supports conditional salvation, and yet it is sometimes used for that purpose.

Revelation 17:14 contains the word *overcome*, but this time it refers to the Lord:

These will make war with the Lamb, and the Lamb will overcome them, for He is Lord of lords and King of kings; and those who are with Him are called, chosen, and faithful.

This verse anticipates Revelation 19:19-21. At the second advent of Christ, the ten kings mentioned in verses 12 and 13 will seek to prevent the Lamb from taking universal dominion. Joined by the heavenly army of all the redeemed, He will overcome them. The words "called, chosen, and faithful" can apply only to saints. Here they are saints who have come *from heaven* with the Lamb (19:14, 21:2). So there is no question of their losing their salvation if they aren't faithful.

Let's consider one more passage about overcoming:

He who overcomes shall inherit all things, and I will be his God and he shall be My son. But the cowardly, unbelieving, abominable, murderers, sexually immoral, sorcerers, idolaters, and all liars shall have their part in the lake which burns with fire and brimstone, which is the second death (Rev. 21:7-8).

There are only two classes, the saved and the lost. Verse 7 describes the saved. All the rest (v. 8) are lost. We are not saved by overcoming. We overcome because we are saved. The one who overcomes inherits all things; eternal life is included in all things. God becomes our Father and we become His sons and daughters when we trust Christ. But the words, "I will be his God and he shall

162

be My son," describe a deeper intimacy of the relationship (cf. 2 Cor. 6:17-18).

ENDNOTES

1 The form here is actually a present *participle,* literally "the believing one." See endnote number 3 in the section on *Eternal Life or Non-Eternal?*

2 John F. MacArthur, *The Glory of Heaven.* Wheaton, IL: Crossway Books, 1996, pp. 99-100.

28
Context or Pretext?

One of the basic rules of interpretation is that a verse or passage must be studied in its context. That is why we say, "A text out of context becomes a pretext."

As an example, take the following:

Now the Spirit of God came upon Azariah the son of Oded. And he went out to meet Asa, and said to him: "Hear me, Asa, and all Judah and Benjamin. The Lord is with you while you are with Him. If you seek Him, He will be found by you; but if you forsake Him, He will forsake you" (2 Chron. 15:1-2).

These verses are sometimes taken out of context to prove that a believer is eternally secure only as long as he seeks the Lord, etc. But the passage is not talking about the salvation of the soul. Asa and his men were jubilant over their recent *military* success! Azariah reminds them that the key to their victory was their faithfulness to the Lord.

Ezekiel 33:7-8 is also taken out of context in an effort to support conditional salvation:

So you, son of man: I have made you a watchman for the house of Israel; therefore you shall hear a word from My mouth and warn them for Me. When I say to the wicked, "O wicked man, you shall surely die!" and you do not speak to warn the wicked from his way, that wicked man shall die in his iniquity; but his blood I will require at your hand.

God appointed Ezekiel as a watchman to warn the people what will happen when He brings the sword upon the land (v. 2), in other words, in time of war. The wicked will die (meaning physical death). However, if the prophet is faithful in warning, he will not be guilty of their blood.

There is no suggestion here that a true believer may subsequently be lost. That idea is quite foreign to the passage. The subject is the responsibility of a watchman to warn the wicked. If a wicked man does not repent, he becomes a war casualty.

In John 15:1-8, the Lord Jesus gave His classic message on the true Vine and the branches. As explained elsewhere, Arminians use verses 2 and 6 to support conditional security. They forget that the theme of the passage is *fruitbearing,* not salvation! If they would put that key in the door, the difficulties would vanish.

Paul spoke of the possibility of his becoming a "castaway" (KJV) or disqualified (1 Cor. 9:27). But the context clearly reveals that he is talking about service, not eternal life. If you don't see this, then Paul's eventual salvation depended on his disciplining his body, and this would be salvation by works.

In studying the book of Hebrews, it's important to see that the context has to do with apostasy, not backsliding. A backslider can be restored; an apostate cannot.

Additional examples of the importance of interpreting a verse in the light of the surrounding verses are given in other chapters. We all need to obey this cardinal rule of Bible interpretation.

29
Position or Practice?

Some of the verses that are used to attack eternal security are clarified when we remember the distinction between a believer's *position* and his *practice,* between his *standing* and his *state.*

When a sinner is converted, God henceforth sees him in Christ. He accepts him, not because of what he is in himself, but because he is in the Beloved. Because a believer is in Christ, he is complete, that is, he does not need anything else to make him fit for heaven. He has a perfect standing before God, not because of any merit of his own, but solely because of the merits of Christ. He is as near to God as Christ is, and loved by the Father as Christ is.

This standing is reached by grace through faith, apart from any meritorious works. And once it is reached, it can never be forfeited. Christ would have to lose his position of acceptance with God before the child of God could.

But then there is the Christian's practice. This refers to his everyday life. Just as his position is what he is in Christ, so his practice is what he is in himself. It is as if the Lord says, "Look, I have saved you by My grace. Now go out and live (with the resources I have given you) in a manner that is worthy of your high calling. I want your practice to be in harmony with your position. The more that is true in your life, the more I will reward you."

God knows that our practice will never perfectly correspond to our position in this life. Our state will never match our standing until we see the Savior and become like Him. But God's will is that we should grow in likeness to Christ while we are here on earth. This is known as progressive sanctification.

This explains the many exhortations to holiness in the New Testament. They are not commandments with the threat of eternal doom attached. Rather, they are instructions in righteousness for those who have been saved by grace. They are practical ways in which we can make our practice harmonize with our position.

This is God's method for producing holiness. Grace says, "I give you a perfect position as a gift of grace. Now, out of love to the Savior who died to make it possible, live in a manner that is worthy of this position."

Law, by contrast, says, "Earn and keep your position by deeds of merit (impossible), and if you don't, you are doomed."

Now let's see how this clarifies some rather difficult passages:

11 *Likewise you also, reckon yourselves to be dead indeed to sin, but alive to God in Christ Jesus our Lord.* 12 *Therefore do not let sin reign in your mortal body, that you should obey it in its lusts.* 13 *And do not present your members as instruments of unrighteousness to sin, but present yourselves to God as being alive from the dead, and your members as instruments of righteousness to God.* 14 *For sin shall not have dominion over you, for you are not under law but under grace.* 15 *What then? Shall we sin because we are not under law but under grace? Certainly not!* 16 *Do you not know that to whom you present yourselves slaves to obey, you are that one's slaves whom you obey, whether of sin leading to death, or of obedience leading to righteousness?* 17 *But God be thanked that though you were slaves of sin, yet you obeyed from the heart that form of doctrine to which you were delivered.* 18 *And having been set free from sin, you became slaves of righteousness.* 19 *I speak in human terms because of the weakness of your flesh. For just as you presented your members as slaves of uncleanness, and of lawlessness leading to more lawlessness, so now present your members as slaves of righteousness for holiness.* 20 *For when you were slaves of sin, you were free in regard to righteousness.* 21 *What fruit did you have then in the things of which you are now ashamed? For the end of those things is death.* 22 *But now having been set free*

from sin, and having become slaves of God, you have your fruit to holiness, and the end, everlasting life. 23 For the wages of sin is death, but the gift of God is eternal life in Christ Jesus our Lord (Rom. 6:11-23).

In the first ten verses of this chapter, the apostle Paul has been speaking about our position. We died to sin (v. 2). Our old man was crucified with Him (v. 6). We have been freed from sin [as master] (v. 7). Since we died with Christ, we shall also live with Him (v. 8).

The rest of the chapter has largely to do with our practice. Since we died to sin positionally, we should reckon ourselves to be dead to sin, that is, by responding to sin as a dead person would (v. 11). Since we have been freed from sin as master, we should live as those who are slaves of righteousness (vv. 13, 16).

It seems strange that the last verse of the chapter would be used to support conditional salvation. The reasoning goes like this: The chapter is obviously written to Christians. Why would Paul warn them that the wages of sin is death if they couldn't lose their salvation and perish?

This completely misses the apostle's line of teaching! He has been contrasting what his readers were before conversion with what they now are by grace. They were slaves of sin; now they are slaves of righteousness. They were slaves of uncleanness, and of lawlessness leading to more lawlessness; now they are to be slaves of righteousness for holiness. They were slaves of sin; now they are slaves of God. To complete the contrast, he reminds them that before they came to Christ, they were earning the wages of sin, namely, death. Now as believers they enjoy the gift of God, namely, eternal life in Christ Jesus our Lord. He is not trying to prove that spiritual death may be their eternal destiny, but stating that eternal life is their portion now and forever.

In fact, the passage actually describes one of the strongest reasons why our salvation is secure. We cannot sin away our salvation, because we have been born again and it is no longer our inclination to sin. Spurgeon comments:

169

...Through the influence of Christ's death upon our souls, *the Holy Ghost has made us now to be actually "dead to sins":* that is to say, we no longer love them, and they have ceased to hold dominion over us. Sin is no longer at home in our hearts; if it enters there, it is an intruder. We are no more its willing servants. Sin calls to us by temptation, but we give it no answer, for we are dead to its voice. Sin promises us a high reward, but we do not consent, for we are dead to its allurements. We sin, but our will is not to sin. It would be heaven to us to be perfectly holy. Our heart and life go after perfection, but sin is abhorred of our soul. "Now, if I do that which I would not, it is no more I that do it, but sin that dwelleth in me." Our truest and most real self loathes sin; and though we fall into it, it is a fall—we are out of our element, and escape from the evil with all speed. The newborn life within us has no dealings with sin; it is dead to sin.[1]

Verse 14 should be conclusive: "For sin shall not have dominion over you, for you are not under law but under grace." Unconverted people are under law. The law tells them what to do, gives them no power to obey, and curses them if they fail. Grace tells them what to do, gives them the power to do it, and rewards them for doing it. If sin is master, then the person has not been born again. Christ is Master of all who are children of God.

Abide in Me, and I in you. As the branch cannot bear fruit of itself, unless it abides in the vine, neither can you, unless you abide in Me (Jn. 15:4).

And now, little children, abide in Him, that when He appears, we may have confidence and not be ashamed before Him at His coming (1 Jn. 2:28).

We have already seen that a Christian's position before God is summed up in the words "in Christ," "in Him," or "in the Beloved." He has no merit of his own as far as fitness for heaven is concerned. But in Christ, he is perfectly fit, and it is this that qualifies him for the Father's home.

As a branch in the true Vine, the believer is responsible to abide in Christ. This means to stay in fellowship with Him, to confess and forsake all known sin, and to obey His Word. Only in this way can he bear fruit for God, have an effective prayer life, glorify the Father, become a disciple in a more ideal sense, and experience fullness of joy. But even after all this, he has to remember that without Christ, he can do nothing.

Sometimes the word "abide" and various forms of the word are descriptive of all true believers. This is their position before God. He sees them as abiding in Christ. At other times they describe what their practice should be. They should abide in Christ as a branch abides in the vine.

First of all, then, let us examine verses that speak of abiding as something that is true of every child of God.

He who says he abides in Him ought himself also to walk just as He walked (1 Jn. 2:6).

In this verse abiding in Him is equivalent to being born again. Anyone who claims to be a Christian should walk as the Savior walked here on earth. Of course, it is also true that if a child of God professes to walk in fellowship with the Lord, he should walk accordingly. But the first interpretation is preferable because in verses 3-5, John is contrasting unbelievers and believers.

He who loves his brother abides in the light, and there is no cause for stumbling in him (1 Jn. 2:10).

Here again the apostle differentiates between the unsaved ("he who hates his brother") and the saved ("he who loves his brother"). The unsaved is in darkness. The saved abides in the light.

Whoever abides in Him does not sin. Whoever sins has neither seen Him nor known Him (1 Jn. 3:6).

The one who abides in the Lord here is a believer. That is his position. We know this because only those who possess divine life are free from the dominion of sin. This is made clear in verse 9: "Whoever has been born of God does not sin," that is, does not practice sin, is not controlled by sin, does not go on sinning. Verses 6 and 9 both speak of the same person.

God says, in effect, to each of His children, "I see you as abiding in Christ; that is your standing or position. But then He quickly adds, "I want you to abide in Christ. That is your state or practice."

> *Abide in Me, and I in you. As the branch cannot bear fruit of itself, unless it abides in the vine, neither can you, unless you abide in Me. I am the vine, you are the branches. He who abides in Me, and I in him, bears much fruit; for without Me you can do nothing...If you abide in Me, and My words abide in you, you will ask what you desire, and it shall be done for you...If you keep My commandments, you will abide in My love, just as I have kept My Father's commandments and abide in His love* (Jn. 15:4, 5, 7, 10).

Whenever the word "abide" is used in these verses, the subject is practice, not position. Exhortations such as the one in verse 4 always refer to how the believer's daily life should harmonize with his position. The one who abides in the Vine (v. 5) is a believer who walks obediently in fellowship with the Lord. The one who abides in Christ and in whom Christ's Word abides (v. 7) is a Christian who lives close to the Lord Jesus.

Obedience is a mark of true sonship (v. 10). It was true of the Savior as a Man here on earth and it should characterize all God's sons and daughters.

> *Therefore let that abide in you which you heard from the beginning. If what you heard from the beginning abides in you, you also will abide in the Son and in the Father...But the anointing which you have received from Him abides in you, and you do not need that anyone teach you; but as the same anointing teaches you concerning all things, and is true, and is not a lie, and just as it has taught you, you will abide in Him. And now, little children, abide in Him, that when He appears, we may have confi-*

dence and not be ashamed before Him at His coming (1 Jn. 2:24, 27, 28).

In verses 24 and 28, to abide is clearly an exhortation. Verse 27 is sometimes translated as an imperative ("abide in Him") and sometimes as an assurance ("you will abide in Him"). In either case, it is speaking of practice, not position. Our position is never dependent on our performance.

The subject of abiding is taken up in greater detail in the notes on John 15 in the chapter entitled "Fruitbearing or Salvation?"

ENDNOTE

1   Charles Haddon Spurgeon, *Till He Come,* Houston, TX: Christian Focus Publications, 1989, p. 339.

30
Deceived or Damned?

Can a born-again Christian be deceived? Obviously, yes. There are several warnings against deception which are addressed to God's people. But does it necessarily follow that if a saint is deceived, he is necessarily doomed or damned? Obviously not.

Believers tend to be gullible. Perhaps because of the Bible's emphasis on faith, they forget that faith demands the surest evidence and finds it in the Word of God. We must not believe every passing wind of doctrine or accept every religious fad or novelty.

With the coming of TV, people are especially open game for deception. Computerized graphics can create lifelike situations and even "miracles." The line between reality and fiction is hard to detect.

Jesus warned His disciples about the advent of false messiahs:

And Jesus answered and said to them, "Take heed that no one deceives you. For many will come in My name, saying, 'I am the Christ,' and will deceive many...Then many false prophets will rise and deceive many. And because lawlessness will abound, the love of many will grow cold. But he who endures to the end shall be saved...Then if anyone says to you, 'Look, here is the Christ!' or 'There!' do not believe it. For false christs and false prophets will rise and show great signs and wonders to deceive, if possible, even the elect. See, I have told you beforehand. Therefore if they say to you, 'Look, He is in the desert!' do not go out; or 'Look, He is in the inner rooms!' do not believe it" (Mt. 24:4-5, 11-13, 23-26).

The fact that these warnings are primarily for Jewish disciples of the Lord Jesus during the Tribulation period does not affect the issue. The fact is that people in any age are subject to deception. Religious leaders who are emissaries of Satan pose as ministers of light. They claim to receive prophecies from God and perform miracles to prove their authenticity. Untaught disciples are easy prey. But disciples can be deluded without denying Christ or losing their salvation.

> *For I am jealous for you with godly jealousy. For I have betrothed you to one husband, that I may present you as a chaste virgin to Christ. But I fear, lest somehow, as the serpent deceived Eve by his craftiness, so your minds may be corrupted from the simplicity that is in Christ. For if he who comes preaches another Jesus whom we have not preached, or if you receive a different spirit which you have not received, or a different gospel which you have not accepted—you may well put up with it! (2 Cor. 11:2-4)*

The Corinthians were in danger of being deceived. Paul had led them to Christ and wanted to rejoice in them at the Judgment Seat of Christ. But false teachers had infiltrated the assembly, seeking to deceive them as the serpent deceived Eve. There was the possibility that they might lose something of their pure and single-hearted devotion to Christ. The Corinthians showed a lovely tolerance of these false apostles. Using irony, Paul chides them for putting out the welcome mat for those who actually were preaching another Jesus, dispensing a different spirit, and proclaiming a different gospel.

There is nothing here to suggest that the Corinthians lost their salvation. They were hoodwinked but had not renounced Christ.

> *Now this I say lest anyone should deceive you with persuasive words. For though I am absent in the flesh, yet I am with you in spirit, rejoicing to see your good order and the steadfastness of your faith in Christ. As you therefore have received Christ Jesus the Lord, so walk in Him, rooted and built up in Him and established in the faith, as you have been taught, abounding in it with*

thanksgiving. Beware lest anyone cheat you through philosophy and empty deceit, according to the tradition of men, according to the basic principles of the world, and not according to Christ (Col. 2:4-8).

When this was written, there were attempts to integrate Christianity with Judaism, intellectualism, asceticism, legalism, and mysticism. Paul warns the Colossians against these errors, just as any faithful under-shepherd would do today. The main difference is that today he might include psychology.

But a warning against deception does not imply that the victim could be lost eternally. Deception does not mean damnation. Think of the deception in the Church today—prosperity theology, the healing racket, false prophecies, and "holy laughter." Many true believers are taken in by these teachings, but it does *not* mean that they lose their salvation.

Paul is not warning the Colossians against the loss of their faith. He rejoices in the steadfastness of their faith and encourages them to continue. They had received the Lord Jesus Christ as Savior by faith (salvation); now they should walk in Him, established in the faith as they had been taught (sanctification).

J. B. Phillips' paraphrase of verse 8 in his *New Testament in Modern English* is especially helpful:

Be careful that no one spoils your faith through intellectualism or high-sounding nonsense. Such stuff is at best founded on men's ideas of the nature of the world, and disregards Christ.

That says it. Faith can be spoiled. It can be adulterated, weakened, or even suffer a temporary lapse. But true faith in Christ will not be renounced.

But evil men and impostors will grow worse and worse, deceiving and being deceived. But you must continue in the things which you have learned and been assured of, knowing from whom you have learned them, and that from childhood you have

177

known the Holy Scriptures, which are able to make you wise for
salvation through faith which is in Christ Jesus (2 Tim. 3:13-15).

The apostle Paul warned Timothy that in the last days deceivers
would go from bad to worse. In contrast to them, Timothy should
continue to abide in God's Word—the sacred Scripture which can
make a person wise for salvation through faith in Christ. This is salvation as a past experience which Timothy had already claimed.
The expression "which are able to make you wise unto salvation"
certainly cannot mean that *Timothy* wasn't already saved. Neither
does it mean that his salvation was contingent on his continued belief. It is simply an adjectival clause, as if to say "the able-to-make-
you-wise-unto-salvation Scriptures." That is one of the many powers of God's Word.

31
Discipline or Destruction?

1 *Moreover, brethren, I do not want you to be unaware that all our fathers were under the cloud, all passed through the sea, 2 all were baptized into Moses in the cloud and in the sea, 3 all ate the same spiritual food, 4 and all drank the same spiritual drink. For they drank of that spiritual Rock that followed them, and that Rock was Christ. 5 But with most of them God was not well pleased, for their bodies were scattered in the wilderness. 6 Now these things became our examples, to the intent that we should not lust after evil things as they also lusted. 7 And do not become idolaters as were some of them. As it is written, "The people sat down to eat and drink, and rose up to play." 8 Nor let us commit sexual immorality, as some of them did, and in one day twenty-three thousand fell; 9 nor let us tempt Christ, as some of them also tempted, and were destroyed by serpents; 10 nor complain, as some of them also complained, and were destroyed by the destroyer. 11 Now all these things happened to them as examples, and they were written for our admonition, upon whom the ends of the ages have come. 12 Therefore let him who thinks he stands take heed lest he fall. 13 No temptation has overtaken you except such as is common to man; but God is faithful, who will not allow you to be tempted beyond what you are able, but with the temptation will also make the way of escape, that you may be able to bear it. 14 Therefore, my beloved, flee from idolatry. 15 I speak as to wise men; judge for yourselves what I say. 16 The cup of blessing which we bless, is it not the communion of the blood of Christ? The bread which we break, is it not the communion of the body of Christ? 17 For we, though many, are one*

bread and one body; for we all partake of that one bread. 18 Ob-
*serve Israel after the flesh: Are not those who eat of the sacri-
fices partakers of the altar?* 19 *What am I saying then? That an
idol is anything, or what is offered to idols is anything?*
20 *Rather, that the things which the Gentiles sacrifice they sacrifice to demons and not to God, and I do not want you to have fellowship with demons.* 21 *You cannot drink the cup of the Lord
and the cup of demons; you cannot partake of the Lord's table
and of the table of demons* (1 Cor. 10:1-21).

This passage has been a happy hunting ground for those who try
to disprove eternal security! The argument seems simple. It was
written to believers and tells how God's people sinned grievously in
the wilderness. As a result God destroyed them. Therefore believers
today can lose their salvation through sin.

The fallacy of the argument is that it fails to distinguish between
God's discipline of *His people in this life* and His eternal punishment of the *wicked in the world to come.* Let us review the passage
with this in mind.

The first four verses tell of the wonderful privileges that the people enjoyed—divine guidance, protection, a God-appointed leader,
an unfailing supply of food and drink. But privileges bring responsibilities. All the soldiers 20 years or older who left Egypt died in the
wilderness except Joshua and Caleb. But this does *not* mean that all
who died perished *eternally!* Moses, Aaron, and Miriam certainly
didn't. God's discipline kept them out of Canaan, but it didn't keep
them out of heaven.

The sins of the Israelites are listed in verses 6-10—lusting for
meat and the foods of Egypt, idolatry, sexual immorality, tempting
the Lord, and complaining. The fact that this history is written as
examples and warnings for us raises the question, "Can a true Christian commit these sins?"

Unfortunately the answer is, Yes! A believer can commit any of
the sins against which he is warned in the New Testament. And if
any such sin is unconfessed, it will incur the Lord's discipline and

keep the person from the place of blessing. If anyone's life is dominated by sin, if his lifestyle is habitually and characteristically sinful, it is evidence that he has never been indwelt by the Holy Spirit. He has never been born again. A Christian may have a besetting sin over which he agonizes, but that is quite different from a life of sinning with the full consent of the will.

No one should think that he has reached the pinnacle of holiness or that he is immune from falling into sin. He is never safe from falling into temptation until he is home in heaven. Every believer is exposed to temptation from within and without. But he is not a helpless victim. Our faithful God limits its intensity and makes an escape route.

The rest of the chapter addresses the carelessness of new converts to sever ties with their idolatrous past. After urging them to flee from idolatry, he gives strong reasons why they should.

It is important to remember that there is a difference between God's judging of a believer and His condemnation of the world. Paul brings out this difference in 1 Corinthians 11:31-32.

For if we would judge ourselves, we would not be judged. But when we are judged, we are chastened by the Lord, that we may not be condemned with the world.

Before we participate in the Lord's Supper, we should judge all known sin in our lives by confessing it and receiving God's forgiveness. If we would do this, we would not be judged by the Lord. The nature of this judgment is given in verse 30—sickness and even death. This is described as the Lord's chastening, a form of parental discipline. Better to endure this chastening than to be among those who suffer eternal condemnation. If we don't experience His chastening, we are not His sons but illegitimate children (Heb. 12:7-8). Verse 32 does not imply that a believer could ever be condemned with the world. Rather it is saying that there are only two possibilities: chastening now, which is the lot of true believers, or condemnation with the world, which is the lot of the unsaved.

32

Additional Passages Used to Support Conditional Salvation

In this section, we will examine various other passages sometimes used to support the conditional view of salvation. Most of these are not central to their arguments, but it will still be profitable to examine them and see whether they do indeed have any bearing on the question.

The first of these is Romans 11:22.

Therefore consider the goodness and severity of God: on those who fell, severity; but toward you, goodness, if you continue in His goodness. Otherwise you also will be cut off.

The final words in this verse, "you also will be cut off," taken out of context, seem to offer positive proof that a believer can subsequently be lost. But if we are going to be careful students of the Bible, we must interpret it in its setting: Who were being addressed and what is meant by being "cut off?"

Let's see the flow of thought in the chapter. The subject is Israel's future. In the first nine verses, Paul teaches that God has cast off Israel, but not completely. The apostle himself is proof that God has reserved a remnant of believing Israelites.

Verses 11 and 12 confirm the fall of Israel, but insist that it's not final. The nation will be restored. In the meantime, the Gentiles have been brought into a place of blessing.

It's important to remember the context. These verses were *not written to individual Christians* or to the *Church*. Paul makes this clear in verse 13, "For I speak to you Gentiles...." In saying this, he distinguishes Gentiles from Jews and from the Church of God (1 Cor. 10:32).

Now he uses the figure of an olive tree with natural branches and then with wild olive branches. The trunk of the tree is *God's line of privilege down through the ages.* It's most important to see this. The trunk is not Israel. It is a *place of favor* in God's dealing with people. Israel, the natural branches, originally held that place as God's chosen, earthly people. But because of unbelief, the nation was "cast off" or "broken off" from its privileged position, and the Gentiles (wild olive branches) were grafted in. They have become what we might call His favored nation. Christ finds more faith among the Gentiles than He does among the people of Israel (Mt. 8:10; 15:28). In that sense, the Gentiles stand by faith. Because the Jewish people judged themselves unworthy of eternal life (Acts 13:46), God sent His salvation to the Gentiles (Acts 28:28).

But the Gentiles should not take their privileged position for granted. If they don't continue to exhibit a relative openness to the Word of the Lord, they will be cut off. This does not mean that saved Gentiles will lose their salvation, but rather that Gentile people as a whole will lose their place of privilege.

We know from other Scriptures that this is exactly what will happen. The wild olive branches (Gentiles) will be cut off and believing Israel will regain their place of privilege before God.

We next turn to a passage in which confusion arises in a different way. We saw earlier in the book that the word *save* has a broad range of meaning; it doesn't always mean the saving of the soul from hell. The word *destroy* can also have various meanings, as we see here:

Yet if your brother is grieved because of your food, you are no longer walking in love. Do not destroy with your food the one for whom Christ died. Therefore do not let your good be spoken of as evil; for the kingdom of God is not eating and drinking, but righteousness and peace and joy in the Holy Spirit. For he who serves Christ in these things is acceptable to God and approved by men. Therefore let us pursue the things which make for peace and the things by which one may edify another. Do not destroy the work of God for the sake of food. All things indeed are pure, but it is evil for the man who eats with offense. It is good neither to eat meat nor drink wine nor do anything by which your brother stumbles or is offended or is made weak. Do you have faith? Have it to yourself before God. Happy is he who does not condemn himself in what he approves. But he who doubts is condemned if he eats, because he does not eat from faith; for whatever is not from faith is sin (Rom. 14:15-23).

First of all, the general teaching of the passage: Paul is dealing with *matters of moral indifference* such as the eating of meats and the observance of days. There was potential among Jewish believers and Gentile believers for a clash on these subjects. So the apostle says that while a person may have Christian liberty in these areas, he shouldn't use it if it would stumble someone else. And if a brother has a bad conscience about eating pork, yet goes ahead and eats it anyway, he has sinned, because whatever can't be done in faith is sin.

The problem arises because of the word *destroy* in verses 15 and 20. "Do not destroy with your food the one for whom Christ died" (v. 15). "Do not destroy the work of God for the sake of food" (v. 20). This does *not* mean to bring about his eternal doom. Instead, it means to stumble him and hinder his spiritual progress. It means to wreck the work which God is doing in the person's life. The man with the weak conscience doesn't lose his salvation, but his spiritual well-being is adversely affected.

Now we consider yet another verse sometimes used by Arminians to support their case.

Not that we have dominion over your faith, but are fellow workers for your joy; for by faith you stand (2 Cor. 1:24).

This verse, especially, the last five words, is used to teach that continued salvation is contingent on continued faith. We are only saved when we keep believing.

Paul is saying something quite different. In speaking frankly to the Corinthians, he was not trying to control their lives. His aim was their joy. As far as their faith was concerned, they were standing firm. It was not their doctrine he was correcting but their behavior. We see more of this in our next passage:

Lest, when I come again, my God will humble me among you, and I shall mourn for many who have sinned before and have not repented of the uncleanness, fornication, and lewdness which they have practiced. This will be the third time I am coming to you. "By the mouth of two or three witnesses every word shall be established." I have told you before, and foretell as if I were present the second time, and now being absent I write to those who have sinned before, and to all the rest, that if I come again I will not spare—since you seek a proof of Christ speaking in me, who is not weak toward you, but mighty in you. For though He was crucified in weakness, yet he lives by the power of God. For we also are weak in Him, but we shall live with Him by the power of God toward you. Examine yourselves as to whether you are in the faith. Test yourselves. Do you not know yourselves, that Jesus Christ is in you?—unless indeed you are disqualified (2 Cor. 12:21-13:5).

Sad to say, believers can commit the three sins mentioned in 12:21. The apostle does not say that they are damned to hell. But he does forewarn them that when he comes to Corinth, he will not spare them, but will discipline them on the basis of the testimony of two or three witnesses.

In saying this, he was conscious that certain teachers had persuaded some of the Corinthians that he was not a true apostle. So he says, "Since you seek a proof of Christ speaking in me...examine yourselves as to whether you are in the faith." (The last part of verse 3 and all of verse 4 are a parenthesis.) The *Corinthians themselves* were proof that he was an apostle. It was he who had led them to the Lamb of God (1 Cor. 9:2) and it was he who had served as a spiritual father to them. So he says, "Prove yourselves. Do you not know yourselves, that Jesus Christ is in you?—unless indeed you are disqualified. But I trust that you will know that we are not disqualified" (vv. 5b-6). If Christ was not in them, they did not pass the test of being believers. But they knew that Christ was in them, and it happened through the ministry of Paul. So he was not disqualified as an apostle after all.

Next we turn to Paul's letter to the Galatians. In it, he was correcting a different problem: the heresy of salvation by works:

You have become estranged from Christ, you who attempt to be justified by law; you have fallen from grace (Gal. 5:4).

This has been a favorite proof text for those who believe in conditional salvation. They quote it to show that when a Christian sins, he falls from grace, and therefore is no longer saved.[1] But is this what the passage says?

It is clear that the apostle is not talking to Christians. The expression "you who attempt to be justified by law" proves that they had never been justified. They were still seeking to be reckoned righteous by God. And they were seeking it in a wrong way, a way in which they would never find it, because it is impossible to be justified by law-keeping. "Therefore by the deeds of the law no flesh will be justified in His sight, for by the law is the knowledge of sin" (Rom. 3:20).

Those who seek to be justified by legal observances have become estranged from Christ. This does not mean that they were once in Christ and then were severed from Him. Rather it means that they cut themselves off from any benefit they might receive from Christ. They must choose between the Lord and the law. To choose one cuts a person off from the other. It must be one or the other; it can't be both. Christ must be all or nothing.

Some might wonder why Paul addresses unsaved people in a letter that is ostensibly to Christians. The apostle was a realist. He knew that in many, if not most, assemblies there was a "mixed multitude," true believers and people who had never been born again.

This was especially true in the churches of Galatia; they had been subverted by false teachers who promoted a false gospel. So he did not hesitate to include unbelievers among his readers.

Our next verse, Ephesians 3:17, is used by conditional security advocates in much the same way as 2 Corinthians 1:24, discussed above:

That Christ may dwell in your hearts through faith... (Eph. 3:17a).

This is wrongly taken to mean that Christ dwells in our hearts only as long as we continue to believe. This is fallacious in two important points.

First of all, once Christ has taken up residence[2] in the life of a believer, He never leaves. He promised, "I will never leave you nor forsake you" (Heb. 13:5b). And again, "...lo, I am with you always, even to the end of the age" (Mt. 28:20).

Second, the idea of a true Christian deciding that he would stop believing is foreign to Scripture. We are saved by faith, and we live by faith (Gal. 2:20). He who gives us eternal life as a free gift guarantees to keep us to enjoy it forever.

If our salvation depended on our faithful continuance, it would be of negative value. But when it is of God alone, it is absolutely sure.

In Paul's letters to Timothy, several passages arise in which Paul instructed Timothy about the dangers of wrong living and false teaching. What exactly were these dangers? Let's see:

But if anyone does not provide for his own, and especially for those of his household, he has denied the faith and is worse than an unbeliever (1 Tim. 5:8).

When there are widows in an assembly who need someone to care for them, this responsibility falls first on the members of their own household or other relatives. If anyone refuses to support a widowed relative, he has denied the faith, and is worse than an unbeliever.

In what sense has he denied the faith? He has acted in a manner that is totally at odds with all that the Christian faith teaches. It does not say that he has thrown over his own faith. He has behaved in an unloving, uncaring, and selfish way.

In what sense is he worse than an unbeliever? In this particular respect: unbelievers generally take care of their own loved ones who are destitute. They show a more humane attitude than this irresponsible Christian.

The verse has nothing to do with the believer's salvation. There is no suggestion that he could lose it by failing to support his widowed mother. However, Paul's stinging rebuke should wake him up "to get his act together."

But those who desire to be rich fall into temptation and a snare, and into many foolish and harmful lusts which drown men in destruction and perdition. For the love of money is a root of all kinds of evil, for which some have strayed from the faith in their greediness, and pierced themselves through with many sorrows. But you, O man of God, flee these things and pursue righteousness, godliness, faith, love, patience, gentleness. Fight the good fight of faith, lay hold on eternal life, to which you were also called and have confessed the good confession in the presence of many witnesses (1 Tim. 6:9-12).

In warning Timothy against the love of money, Paul says that those who desire to be rich fall into lusts which drown men in destruction and perdition. These latter words do *not* mean loss of being but loss of *well*-being. They indicate ruin as far as the purpose of their creation is concerned. For a believer, they could mean the loss of his family, money, home, and testimony. They could include imprisonment as well for graft, bribery, embezzlement, and theft.

The love of money causes some to stray from the faith. They become backsliders, leaving the highway of holiness to wander in the fields of sin. While they do not deny the fundamentals of the Christian faith, they do live in a manner that is not worthy of the gospel. They may still have faith and yet not walk by faith as they should.

189

Young Timothy should not be such a contradiction, but should adorn the doctrine. He should lay hold of eternal life by "practically appropriating all the benefits, privileges, and responsibilities involved in the possession of it" (W.E. Vine).

There is nothing in verse 12 to suggest that Timothy could lay hold of eternal life by his character or works. He already had it, but was encouraged to enjoy it to the maximum in the here and now.

Command those who are rich in this present age not to be haughty, nor to trust in uncertain riches but in the living God, who gives us richly all things to enjoy. Let them do good, that they be rich in good works, ready to give, willing to share, storing up for themselves a good foundation for the time to come, that they may lay hold on eternal life (1 Tim. 6:17-19).

Here wealthy Christians are taught to lay hold of eternal life, not by hoarding their money but by doing good, by being rich in good works, "ready to give, willing to share." This is not salvation by works but works as the fruit of salvation.

O Timothy! Guard what was committed to your trust, avoiding the profane and idle babble and contradictions of what is falsely called knowledge—by professing it some have strayed concerning the faith (1 Tim. 6:20-21a).

Again Paul resorts to the figure of straying from the faith. Some of the Christians in Ephesus had swallowed "profane and idle babblings and contradictions of what is falsely called knowledge." To be occupied with godless chatter and the contradictory teachings that falsely pose as knowledge is to miss the mark or err as far as the faith is concerned. Again it is not a question of eternal salvation but of being diverted from what is central to doctrinal trivia and insidious questionings.

Flee also youthful lusts; but pursue righteousness, faith, love, peace with those who call on the Lord out of a pure heart. But avoid foolish and ignorant disputes, knowing that they generate

190

strife. And a servant of the Lord must not quarrel but be gentle to all, able to teach, patient, in humility correcting those who are in opposition, if God perhaps will grant them repentance, so that they may know the truth, and that they may come to their senses and escape the snare of the devil, having been taken captive by him to do his will (2 Tim. 2:22-26).

Verses 25 and 26 supposedly demonstrate that saved people can forfeit their salvation by falling into the devil's trap. Is this really what it says? The passage tells Timothy how to deal with those who promote foolish and ignorant disputes in the assembly. They are pawns of Satan to generate strife and disunity. Timothy should deal with them patiently, humbly, and graciously. Hopefully they will repent of their pushy foolishness and recognize the truth of the matters under dispute. They will then realize that they have acted as agents of the devil, helping him in his evil work of creating division among God's people.

Again, the passage does not prove that saved people can be lost, but it shows that they can cause strife over trivial matters and thus promote Satan's agenda.

James wrote his letter to an audience of professing believers. Unfortunately, many of them were living lives that made their salvation questionable. Therefore it is not surprising that his letter contains some sharply-worded warnings:

Blessed is the man who endures temptation; for when he has been approved, he will receive the crown of life which the Lord has promised to those who love Him. Let no one say when he is tempted, "I am tempted by God"; for God cannot be tempted by evil, nor does He Himself tempt anyone. But each one is tempted when he is drawn away by his own desires and enticed. Then, when desire has conceived, it gives birth to sin; and sin, when it is full-grown, brings forth death (Jas. 1:12-15).

In verse 12, James may be speaking both of holy *trials* and unholy *temptations*. It's the same word in the original language. The one who endures these is rewarded with the crown of life, not eternal life. It is a question of rewards, not salvation.

Verses 13-15 clearly speak of unholy temptations. These do not come from God but from man's fallen nature.

James likens the course of sin to human life—conception, birth, growth, and finally death. He does not imply that every time a Christian sins, he dies. Didn't Jesus promise that the one who eats the bread that comes down from heaven would not die (Jn. 6:50), that whoever lives and believes in Him would never die (Jn. 11:26)?

James knew very well that a person can be a believer and yet sin. Why then did he warn that sin eventually ends in death? He did it to remind his readers of the enormity of sin. In the case of true believers, their sins resulted in the death of their Divine Substitute. The moment they trusted Christ, they died in Him. In the case of those who die outside of Christ, their sins result in eternal death. So death is always the wages of sin (Rom. 6:23), either the death of a Substitute or the death of the sinner.

If someone claims to be saved and yet his life is dominated by sin, he shows that his profession is false. He never was a believer, and unless he repents and believes in Christ, his doom is sealed.

> *Adulterers and adulteresses! Do you not know that friendship with the world is enmity with God? Whoever therefore wants to be a friend of the world makes himself an enemy of God. Or do you think that the Scripture says in vain, "The Spirit who dwells in us yearns jealously"? But He gives more grace. Therefore He says: "God resists the proud, but gives grace to the humble." Therefore submit to God. Resist the devil and he will flee from you. Draw near to God and He will draw near to you. Cleanse your hands, you sinners; and purify your hearts, you double-minded. Lament and mourn and weep! Let your laughter be turned to mourning and your joy to gloom. Humble yourselves in the sight of the Lord, and He will lift you up (Jas. 4:4-10).*

The question naturally arises, "To whom is James speaking in these verses—Christians or non-believers?" The answer is that he is purposely ambiguous. James is a "show me" disciple. He wants evidence to support a person's claim to faith, because "faith without works is dead" (2:26).

Would he address real believers as adulteresses? He well might. Sometimes it is necessary to use strong language to wake people up. I remember once when Dr. Donald Grey Barnhouse was addressing Christians in Chicago about conditions in that city, he thundered, "And whose fault is it? It's yours, you ungodly fundamentalists!" He was using hyperbole, or effective exaggeration, to shock the Christians into action.

So James is warning people against friendship with the world. It is enmity against God. And if the shoe fits, put it on.

Verse 5 is difficult. Let me give two common interpretations.

1. Do you think that the indwelling Holy Spirit would ever cause or condone the desire for friendship with the world?

2. Do you think that the Scripture says in vain that the Holy Spirit yearns jealously for our undivided devotion to the Lord? (No verse in the Bible says that in so many words, but it is certainly the tenor of the Scriptures.)

Neither explanation is relevant to our discussion of eternal security. The fact is that we, as believers, are attracted and influenced by the world more than we would care to admit. Somewhere there is a line which, when passed, makes a person a lover of the world. No one knows where that line is. Christians should stay as far from it as possible.

In the spiritual battles of life, God gives grace to those who are not self-confident or arrogant. So we should submit to God and say "No!" to the devil. When we walk in fellowship with the Lord, we can be sure of His special nearness.

In verse 8b, James addresses his readers as sinners and double-minded. Could these adjectives be true of children of God? Yes! Sinners here are people whose hands need cleansing, and the double-minded are those whose hearts need purifying. Can Christians be guilty of unclean acts and impure motives? Yes. Well, then, the labels stick!

The last two verses describe genuine repentance and brokenness. They are the road to spiritual recovery.

We next turn to the First Epistle of Peter. He describes the Lord's faithfulness toward us and our responsibility toward Him in this way:

Who are kept by the power of God through faith for salvation ready to be revealed in the last time. In this you greatly rejoice, though now for a little while, if need be, you have been grieved by various trials, that the genuineness of your faith, being much more precious than gold that perishes, though it is tested by fire, may be found to praise, honor, and glory at the revelation of Jesus Christ, whom having not seen you love. Though now you do not see Him, yet believing, you rejoice with joy inexpressible and full of glory, receiving the end of your faith—the salvation of your souls...Therefore gird up the loins of your mind, be sober, and rest your hope fully upon the grace that is to be brought to you at the revelation of Jesus Christ (1 Pet. 1:5-9, 13).

This is a strong passage on the eternal security of the believer. It assures us without any conditions that a glorious inheritance is kept for us and that we are kept for the inheritance. However, those who believe in conditional salvation point to the expression "kept by the power of God through faith unto salvation" and argue that we are only kept as long as we continue to believe. What is the answer?

The idea of a true believer ceasing to believe is purely hypothetical. The Bible knows nothing about it. It is unthinkable that one who is indwelt by Christ could or would drive Him out.

Once a person is saved, he becomes the full responsibility of the Savior, who guarantees that he will never perish. In times of depression and in mental breakdowns, a child of God may doubt his own salvation, but what a comfort to know that he is still held by Jesus' mighty grip!

We do not contribute to our salvation by our faith. Faith is merely the empty hand that receives what God gives us. We are saved by faith and we live by faith (Gal. 2:20). There is nothing meritorious in faith. All the merit is in Christ, the object of faith. So we accept by faith the fact that we are kept by the power of God unto salvation in its future tense, that is, salvation in heaven from the very presence of sin.

In the meantime, we encounter trials which test the genuineness of our faith. It is our faith, not ourselves, that is tested by fire. Proved genuine, it results in praise, honor, and glory to the Lord Jesus and ourselves as well.

We haven't seen Him yet, but faith makes Him real to us and we love Him. Also we are filled with glorious joy as we receive the end of our faith, the salvation of our souls.

In verse 13, the word "hope" is used by Arminians to create uncertainty about our eventual salvation. Here is another place where definitions are crucial. The Christian's hope is the grace that is to be brought to him at the revelation of Jesus Christ, in other words, the glorified state. The hope of this consummation has no doubt or uncertainty connected with it. It is based on the infallible Word of God and is therefore as certain as if it had already taken place.

Finally, our last two passages are both warnings concerning those who tamper with God's Word:

As also in all his [Paul's] *epistles, speaking in them of these things, in which are some things hard to understand, which untaught and unstable people twist to their own destruction, as they do also the rest of the Scriptures. You therefore, beloved, since you know this beforehand, beware lest you also fall from your own steadfastness, being led away with the error of the wicked* (2 Pet. 3:16-17).

Peter describes people who take scriptures dealing with important Bible doctrines and twist them to mean what *they* want them to say. It's a willful distortion of the Word to teach error and it results in their destruction.

Believers are warned against any who handle the Scriptures in this way lest their firm foundation in the faith be shaken and they be defiled by false teachings. There is no thought here of Christians

195

losing their salvation. It is possible to have one's faith adulterated without denying the faith.

For I testify to everyone who hears the words of the prophecy of this book: If anyone adds to these things, God will add to him the plagues that are written in this book; and if anyone takes away from the words of the book of this prophecy, God shall take away his part from the Book of Life, from the holy city, and from the things which are written in this book (Rev. 22:18-19).

It's a serious thing to tamper with the Word of God, either by maliciously adding to it or taking from it. The person who does it is saying that he knows better than God. He is an arrogant unbeliever.

The punishment for adding to the Scriptures is to have its plagues added to the guilty one. The punishment for taking away from the Word is to have one's part taken away from the tree[3] of life, from the holy city, and from the blessings that are written in the Bible.

Anyone can have part in the tree of life by repenting of his sins and receiving Christ as Lord and Savior, but the crass unbelief that seeks to rewrite the Scriptures bars him from access to that part. He cannot claim his part. It is taken away from him. Verse 19 is not describing a hypothetical Christian who ceases to believe but a rank unbeliever who rejects the inspiration and infallibility of the Bible.

ENDNOTES

1   Their teaching is widely known as "the falling away doctrine."

2   It's worth noting that the word *dwell* here is a strengthened form of the verb in the original. It may suggest "settle down" or "feel at home."

3   Most manuscripts have "tree of life" here instead of "book of life," but that doesn't materially affect the subject at hand.

33
What is the Answer?

There is one thing on which both sides of the security problem agree. They share a common concern over the many people who claim to be Christians and yet live in sin. It pains them to see the Name of the Lord Jesus dishonored by lives that are *libels* rather than *Bibles*. They see the fruits of "easy believism," of empty-hearted professions, of what is sometimes called "cheap grace."

Children are put under emotional pressure to "open their hearts' door to Jesus," but in later life they get involved in drugs, alcohol, and sexual immorality. Yet their Christian parents assure them that they were saved when they were young. And some of these same parents react vehemently to any suggestion to the contrary.

Gangsters get "saved" but return to life in the underworld. The media report the conversion of actors and actresses, but these stars never make a break with the world of violent and immoral films. The names of "televangelists" are splashed in the headlines when they are exposed as womanizers or financial racketeers. Evangelicals are delighted when a politician claims to be born again, but the let-down comes when his public utterances are laced with profanity.

A great wave of profession has swept the country. It's often the popular thing to be known as a Christian. Sometimes it's good for a businessman to carry that label. And it's good in politics because it means votes. Christendom has become a kingdom of religious confusion. Anyone who is jealous for the honor of Christ is embarrassed and ashamed.

Although those who believe in eternal security and those who hold to conditional security are united in deploring the loose living among those who say they are Christians, they differ in their analysis of the situation. The conditional salvationists say that these people were saved but lost their salvation. The others say that they were never saved at all. They had nothing but a false profession.

The purpose of this book has been to show that a true believer is eternally secure, and that the contrary view is fallacious for the following reasons:

• It is *unbiblical.* There is nothing in the Bible, rightly understood, that suggests that a true sheep of Christ can ever perish. Not one verse teaches that a justified person might fail to be glorified at last. The consistent testimony of the Word of God is that to be truly born again is to be saved eternally.

• It redefines *eternal* to mean something less than eternal.

• It betrays a defective understanding of the meaning of *grace.* It fails to realize that salvation is completely undeserved, that it is a free gift, and that, once given, it is never retracted.

• It insists that Christ's work on the Cross is not enough, but that man must do his part by persevering, enduring, or overcoming. Thus it makes eventual salvation depend on man's power as well as Christ's. It makes man a co-savior. This is a fatal flaw. The Lord Jesus is the *only* Savior, and He won't share that honor with any creature!

• It tries to *mix grace and works,* which God Himself says is impossible.

• It seems oblivious to the fact that man is no more able to keep himself saved than he was to save himself in the first place.

• It allows for a person to be born again *repeatedly.* This is a fiction that is foreign to the Bible.

• It denies that final salvation takes place at a point in time, insisting that it is a process conditioned on man's fulfilling certain requirements, This conflicts with Jesus' words in John 10:9: "I am the door. If anyone enters by Me, he will be saved, and will go in and out and find pasture." We have only to enter the door once. It is not a revolving-door theology.

• It makes it impossible for anyone to have final assurance of salvation, forgetful that the apostles had it and so did those believers to whom they wrote.

• It allows for boasting in heaven. People could brag about their faithfulness and perseverance. But salvation by grace through faith excludes boasting.

Conditional security has been weighed in the balances and found wanting. The consistent testimony of the Bible is: *Once in Christ, in Christ forever.*

HOW FIRM A FOUNDATION

How firm a foundation, ye saints of the Lord,
Is laid for your faith in His excellent Word!
What more can He say than to you He hath said,
To you, who for refuge to Jesus have fled?

"Fear not, I am with thee, O be not dismayed,
For I am thy God, I will still give thee aid;
I'll strengthen thee, help thee, and cause thee to stand,
Upheld by My gracious, omnipotent hand.

"When through fiery trials thy pathway shall lie,
My grace, all sufficient shall be thy supply;
The flame shall not hurt thee, I only design
Thy dross to consume, and thy gold to refine.

"The soul that on Jesus hath leaned for repose,
I will not, I will not desert to his foes;
That soul, though all hell should endeavor to shake,
I'll never, no never, no never forsake!"

—K in Rippon's *Selection of Hymns,* 1787

SOVEREIGN GRACE O'ER SIN ABOUNDING

Sov'reign grace o'er sin abounding,
Ransomed souls, the tidings swell;
'Tis a deep that knows no sounding,
Who its breadth or length can tell?
On its glories, on its glories
Let my soul forever dwell!

What from Christ the soul can sever,
Bound by everlasting bands?
Once in Him, in Him forever,
Thus th' eternal cov'nant stands.
None shall pluck thee, none shall pluck thee
From the Savior's mighty hands.

Heirs of God, joint-heirs with Jesus,
Long e'er time its race begun:
To His name eternal praises,
O what wonders love has done!
One with Jesus, one with Jesus,
By eternal union one.

On such love, my soul, still ponder,
Love so great, so rich, so free;
Say, while lost in holy wonder,
Why, O Lord, such love to me?
Hallelujah! Hallelujah!
Grace shall reign eternally.

—John Kent

	ETERNAL SECURITY	CONDITIONAL SECURITY
THE GOSPEL	Believe on the Lord Jesus Christ, and you will be saved (Acts 16:31)	Believe on the Lord Jesus Christ, and you will be saved (Acts 16:31).
SALVATION	An instant, complete work of God that is eternal in its result when a sinner repents and believes	Not the act of a moment, but a continuing process of believing by the Christian and keeping from sin.
FAITH	Once a person truly believes on Christ, he never ceases to believe.	A believer can decide that he doesn't want to believe any longer.
SIN	Any sin breaks fellowship with God, but not relationship. If sin dominates a person's life, it indicates that he was never saved.	Sin can break relationship if serious enough and prolonged. A Christian who sins forfeits his salvation. (Nature and extent of sin are not clearly defined.)
ATONEMENT	Christ's death atoned for all a believer's sin—past, present, and future.	Seems to imply that Christ's death atoned for a believer's sins up to the present.
WORKS	Works have no part in obtaining salvation. Works are the fruit of salvation, not the root.	Salvation is not by works but a believer must remain steadfast, endure, persevere, abide, and obey the commandments of the Lord. He must acknowledge the Lordship of Christ in every area of life.
ASSURANCE	Salvation is sure because it is a gift, because Christ has finished the work of redemption, and because the believer is accepted in the Beloved and complete in Him.	Full assurance is not possible because a person never knows if he will continue to the end.
MOTIVE FOR HOLY LIVING	When a person is saved, he doesn't want to sin. God has taken that "want" out of his life, and replaced it with the desire to please the Lord in all things. His motive is love to the Lord who died for him—a much stronger motive than fear.	If a believer were eternally secure, then he could go out and sin all he wants to. This doctrine leads to careless living. Believers must be restrained by the fear of losing their salvation.

Scripture Reference Index

Breinigsville, PA USA
14 September 2010
245373BV00001B/1/A